Teen
Pregnancy

OTHER BOOKS OF RELATED INTEREST

Teen Pregnancy

Myra H. Immell, *Book Editor*

David L. Bender, *Publisher*
Bruno Leone, *Executive Editor*
Bonnie Szumski, *Editorial Director*
Stuart B. Miller, *Managing Editor*
Brenda Stalcup, *Series Editor*

Contemporary Issues
Companion

Greenhaven Press, Inc., San Diego, CA

Every effort has been made to trace the owners of copyrighted material. The articles in this volume may have been edited for content, length, and/or reading level. The titles have been changed to enhance the editorial purpose. Those interested in locating the original source will find the complete citation on the first page of each article.

No part of this book may be reproduced or used in any form or by any means, electrical, mechanical, or otherwise, including, but not limited to, photocopy, recording, or any information storage and retrieval system, without prior written permission from the publisher.

Library of Congress Cataloging-in-Publication Data

Teen pregnancy / Myra H. Immell, book editor.
     p.   cm. — (Contemporary issues companion)
   Includes bibliographical references and index.
   ISBN 0-7377-0465-9 (pbk. : alk. paper) —
ISBN 0-7377-0466-7 (lib. bdg.)
   1. Teenage pregnancy. 2. Teenage mothers. 3. Teenagers—Sexual behavior. 4. Teenage pregnancy—Prevention. 5. Sex instruction for youth. I. Immell, Myra H. II. Series.

HQ759.4 .T423 2001
306.874'3—dc21   00-037136
                                                        CIP

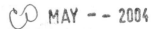 MAY – – 2004

CONTENTS

FOREWORD

In the news, on the streets, and in neighborhoods, individuals are confronted with a variety of social problems. Such problems may affect people directly: A young woman may struggle with depression, suspect a friend of having bulimia, or watch a loved one battle cancer. And even the issues that do not directly affect her private life—such as religious cults, domestic violence, or legalized gambling—still impact the larger society in which she lives. Discovering and analyzing the complexities of issues that encompass communal and societal realms as well as the world of personal experience is a valuable educational goal in the modern world.

Effectively addressing social problems requires familiarity with a constantly changing stream of data. Becoming well informed about today's controversies is an intricate process that often involves reading myriad primary and secondary sources, analyzing political debates, weighing various experts' opinions—even listening to firsthand accounts of those directly affected by the issue. For students and general observers, this can be a daunting task because of the sheer volume of information available in books, periodicals, on the evening news, and on the Internet. Researching the consequences of legalized gambling, for example, might entail sifting through congressional testimony on gambling's societal effects, examining private studies on Indian gaming, perusing numerous websites devoted to Internet betting, and reading essays written by lottery winners as well as interviews with recovering compulsive gamblers. Obtaining valuable information can be time-consuming—since it often requires researchers to pore over numerous documents and commentaries before discovering a source relevant to their particular investigation.

Greenhaven's Contemporary Issues Companion series seeks to assist this process of research by providing readers with useful and pertinent information about today's complex issues. Each volume in this anthology series focuses on a topic of current interest, presenting informative and thought-provoking selections written from a wide variety of viewpoints. The readings selected by the editors include such diverse sources as personal accounts and case studies, pertinent factual and statistical articles, and relevant commentaries and overviews. This diversity of sources and views, found in every Contemporary Issues Companion, offers readers a broad perspective in one convenient volume.

In addition, each title in the Contemporary Issues Companion series is designed especially for young adults. The selections included in every volume are chosen for their accessibility and are expertly edited in consideration of both the reading and comprehension levels

7

of the audience. The structure of the anthologies also enhances accessibility. An introductory essay places each issue in context and provides helpful facts such as historical background or current statistics and legislation that pertain to the topic. The chapters that follow organize the material and focus on specific aspects of the book's topic. Every essay is introduced by a brief summary of its main points and biographical information about the author. These summaries aid in comprehension and can also serve to direct readers to material of immediate interest and need. Finally, a comprehensive index allows readers to efficiently scan and locate content.

The Contemporary Issues Companion series is an ideal launching point for research on a particular topic. Each anthology in the series is composed of readings taken from an extensive gamut of resources, including periodicals, newspapers, books, government documents, the publications of private and public organizations, and Internet websites. In these volumes, readers will find factual support suitable for use in reports, debates, speeches, and research papers. The anthologies also facilitate further research, featuring a book and periodical bibliography and a list of organizations to contact for additional information.

A perfect resource for both students and the general reader, Greenhaven's Contemporary Issues Companion series is sure to be a valued source of current, readable information on social problems that interest young adults. It is the editors' hope that readers will find the Contemporary Issues Companion series useful as a starting point to formulate their own opinions about and answers to the complex issues of the present day.

INTRODUCTION

The staggering rate of teenage pregnancy in the United States is a serious matter of concern. According to recent statistics, more than 900,000 teenage pregnancies occur each year; four in ten American girls will become pregnant at least once during their teens. And while teen pregnancy is also a problem in many other countries, the United States has the highest rate by far among all fully industrialized nations. As of 2000, the U.S. teen pregnancy rate was nearly double Great Britain's, four times higher than in France and Germany, and more than ten times greater than that of Japan.

In the United States, as in most other industrialized countries, teen mothers often find it difficult to complete their education and face the prospect of financial hardship. For example, the National Campaign to Prevent Teen Pregnancy and the National Center for Health reported in the late 1990s that approximately forty thousand teen girls drop out of school each year due to pregnancy. Of mothers between the ages of fifteen and seventeen, 90 percent are not employed and 72 percent are on welfare. Furthermore, the babies of these young mothers typically have more physical problems than children born to older mothers. Tom Kean, the chairperson of the National Campaign to Prevent Teen Pregnancy, notes that babies born to teen mothers are at greater risk for many serious medical conditions, including low birth weight, mental retardation, blindness, deafness, mental illness, cerebral palsy, and infant mortality. Overall, these children tend to receive poorer medical care, contract more childhood illnesses, and experience delayed development at a higher rate than children born to older mothers.

Most teen mothers were themselves born and raised in poverty, and the cycle continues with their children, who tend to suffer more from hunger and malnourishment and be exposed to more violence, abuse, and neglect. They also are more likely to do poorly in school or to drop out entirely. According to Kean, the daughters of teen mothers are 22 percent more likely to become pregnant themselves during their teen years, while the sons of teen mothers are 13 percent more likely to end up in jail.

Teen pregnancy has an impact not just on individual teens and their children but also on the American public in general. For instance, the financial repercussions are felt by every American who pays taxes. Collectively, American taxpayers spend $40 billion a year to support families started by teenage mothers. According to a 1999 report by the Centers for Disease Control and Prevention (CDC), the cost of teenage childbearing to taxpayers during the five-year period between 1985 and 1990 was $120 billion. If these teens had delayed their pregnancies at least until they reached the age of twenty, the CDC maintains, the total expenditure could have been reduced by $48 billion.

The financial repercussions of teenage pregnancy and the dire outlook for the future of teen parents and their children have led many experts and concerned citizens to search for a way to reduce America's high teen pregnancy rates. There is general agreement among most Americans that the key to reducing and preventing teen pregnancies is to change teens' sexual behaviors. Until such a change is effected, little progress can be made in substantially reducing—let alone virtually eliminating—the problem of teen pregnancy. Americans do not agree, however, on the most effective way to go about altering teen sexual behaviors. For example, while many groups and individuals emphasize the importance of sex education in reducing the rate of teen pregnancy, they have differing opinions about exactly what should be taught.

One approach toward sex education is to focus on the importance of abstinence. Abstinence-only programs teach that sex before marriage is wrong and that contraception is not a reliable method for preventing pregnancy or sexually transmitted diseases (STDs). Supporters of the abstinence-only movement often favor excluding information about safe sex, which they believe encourages students to become sexually active. Crystal Wright, a spokesperson for the Best Friends abstinence-only group, explains: "We don't talk about contraception. We feel that when you are teaching a child to say no, teaching contraception negates it. . . . What we teach is that if you postpone sex until your high school graduation, or better yet, until marriage, you're going to have a healthier, happier life." Supporters of the abstinence-only approach argue that these programs are effective in preventing teen pregnancy, as well as encouraging self-restraint and traditional morals among American teens. Researchers, however, indicate that as of yet there is no definitive proof that abstinence-only programs impede, accelerate, or reduce sexual activity.

Critics of the abstinence-only method argue that such programs completely disregard the realities of sexual activity among teenagers and even endanger teens by not teaching safe sex practices. In their view, increasing contraceptive use among teenagers is a viable strategy to help reduce the teen pregnancy rate. They advocate broader-based sex education programs that provide thorough and nonjudgmental information about sexuality, STDs, and contraceptives. Some also promote the establishment of school-based health clinics that distribute condoms and other contraceptives to students. Many experts in youth development prefer a variation of this approach: a wide-ranging sex-education curriculum that includes discussion both of the benefits of delaying sexual activity and the proper use of contraceptives. These broad-based sex education programs have been criticized by proponents of abstinence-only methods as encouraging and enabling teens to become sexually active, but researchers have concluded that these programs do not lead to an increase in sexual activity among teens. On the other hand, the researchers also admit that these programs have not been highly successful in reducing teen pregnancy.

While the various educational strategies to prevent and reduce teen pregnancy have not met with total success, the rate of teenage pregnancy in the United States has in fact been on the decline since the early 1990s. According to the National Center for Health Statistics, between 1991 and 1998 the teen pregnancy rate dropped by 18 percent. In 1999, health officials reported that the percentage of fifteen- to seventeen-year-old girls having babies had dropped to its lowest level in forty years, with the most recent figures showing teen pregnancy lower than any time in the twenty-three years since statistics were first tallied. The decline in the teen pregnancy rate has been across all racial and ethnic groups, but the greatest decrease has been among African American teens, who in the past have had the highest birthrates. According to government figures, in 1999 the birthrate for unmarried African American women fell lower than in any year since 1969. More recently, the highest birthrates have occurred among Hispanic teens.

Experts attribute the overall decline in the rate of teenage pregnancy in the United States to various factors. Among these are a decrease in sexual activity and an increase in the use of birth control. The president of the National Campaign to Prevent Teen Pregnancy credits the downward trend to "less sex, more contraception, and a growing recognition among teens themselves that their focus should be on education and growing up." Secretary of Health and Human Services Donna Shalala cites such factors as fear of AIDS and a rise in the number of teens holding conservative values. Economic factors may also play a role. Some commentators maintain that the resurgent economy has contributed by providing poor teenage girls with more feasible options for their future than early motherhood. Others contend that the welfare reform measures passed in the mid-1990s, which drastically cut the amount of aid available to teen mothers and their children, have forced teens to think harder about taking on the financial obligation inherent in raising a child. In the words of Sarah Brown, director of the National Campaign to Prevent Teen Pregnancy, "teenagers are getting the message that starting families while still young themselves is a situation where everyone loses."

While the recent downward trend is promising, experts agree that teen pregnancy remains an ongoing problem that has by no means been resolved. *Teen Pregnancy: Contemporary Issues Companion* provides a comprehensive examination of the issues and dilemmas surrounding the topic of teenage pregnancy. The authors included in the anthology cover a broad spectrum: Teen pregnancy experts, social workers, health care professionals, journalists, educators, pregnant teens, and teen parents are among the diverse voices represented. In the following chapters, these authors explore the options available to pregnant teens and delve into the personal ramifications of teen pregnancy and parenthood. They also present the factors that contribute to the high rate of teen pregnancy and discuss various measures designed to reduce the occurrence and impact of this serious problem.

CHAPTER 1

THE REALITIES OF TEEN SEXUAL ACTIVITY AND PREGNANCY

Contemporary Issues
Companion

Why Children Are Having Children

Evelyn Lerman

Evelyn Lerman focuses on two issues of concern—young people having sex at a very early age and the related problem of children having children. Lerman contends that there is a strong link between poverty and teen pregnancy. Teen pregnancy also can stem from a number of societal forces, she writes, including the lack of positive male role models, early sexual abuse, and sexual advances by older males. Lerman allows the numerous teens she interviewed to tell in their own words how these and other factors contributed to their lack of self-esteem, feelings of insecurity, and early sexual activity and pregnancy. Lerman is a former teacher and the author of *Teen Moms: The Pain and the Promise,* from which the following selection is excerpted.

Everyone asks the questions. "Why are children having children? What are they doing having sex so early?" You hear it at gatherings, on talk shows, in professional meetings—wherever people are talking about conditions in America today. What is the reason children, some as young as 12, are having sex, and sometimes getting pregnant as a result? The answers are complex. Many theories are expressed by adults who work with teens, by researchers in the field, and by the teens themselves as they tell their stories.

The social workers, psychologists, and educators answer by talking about teen feelings. They cite neglect, abuse, and society's mores as causes. They say loneliness and lack of self-esteem are the result. They talk about peer pressure, absent fathers, single mothers, sexual and physical abuse, alcohol, drugs, male predators and crushing burdens of responsibility on teens. They mention adult role models from movies, TV, and sports having promiscuous sex and bearing children without being married. . . .

The researchers give us an even broader perspective. They talk about trends, trace the history of the United States from 1940 to 1993, and point out the economic realities of the 90s. According to Mike A. Males, author of *The Scapegoat Generation,* these were years of upheaval in sexual mores. He cites a depressed wartime birthrate, the postwar baby boom, the sexual revolution based in part on the widespread use of the birth control pill and the legalization of abortion, the increase in divorce and unwed births, and the steady decrease in the age of puberty. . . .

Poverty with its attendant issues is at the core of the teen childbearing problem. Six out of seven of America's teenage mothers were poor before they gave birth. . . .

Judith S. Musick, who authored *Young, Poor and Pregnant*, attests that poverty is even more influential than race or ethnicity. Adolescents get pregnant from all groups, of course, but it is the teens from lower socioeconomic groups, the children of poverty who do not have other options open to them, who most often deliver and raise their children.

The Importance of Father Absence

The fifty teens I interviewed, unable to discern cause from effect, unaware of the societal and economic forces that were shaping their lives, talked about people. They told me about the men, women, and peers in their lives. Jacqueline . . . and Tracy talked about their absent fathers:

> *Jacqueline, 16*: I think I'm okay emotionally somehow because I've been through a lot in my life, even before this, and I learned how to take it. My parents are divorced, and I live with my mom. My father got a new family and has his wife's two children now.
>
> When he got married again he told my brother and me he'd see us when he sees us. I was seven then. He still brings child support to my mother, and he talks to me when he comes, but I don't think he really cares about me. . . .
>
> *Tracy, 16*: My parents were divorced when I was 8. I don't talk to my dad. My brothers do, but I don't like him and I don't see him. Great-grandpa is 92, and this baby will be the fifth generation in this state.
>
> Great-grandpa is amazing. He makes things from rocks. He's neat. He's very strong still, but I don't know if he's strong enough to hear that I'm pregnant. I haven't told him. . . .
>
> My life was good. So how come I got pregnant at 15? It just happened. The luck of the draw. I was lucky it wasn't earlier because I was 14 when I started having sex. Here in this state the guys are real fast. It's put out or get out. Lots of parties. We didn't do drugs, though.

Each of these teens expressed a sense of loss because she didn't have a father. . . . It appears that whether the absent father shows interest or is totally absent, the perceived loss is real and deep. These young women feel rejected. . . .

Lacking communication with a close, loving, positive male role model, teens approach their sexuality with insecurity and doubt. According to Musick, "The feelings, thoughts, and actions of these adolescent girls can be understood as logical outcomes of their attempts to cope with father absence.". . .

The professionals and researchers agree that the lack of positive male role models is a significant factor in early sex and pregnancy. . . . Males cites "the upsurge in divorce" between 1940 and 1993 as one of the contributing factors in the rise of unwed teenage births.

We know there are fathers who, in spite of divorce, support their families with both emotional and financial assistance, and that the daughters of these families can grow up whole and secure. But the overwhelming number of divorced fathers of adolescents, especially among the teen mother population, do not provide child care or child support, and the children suffer the consequences.

The Threat of Sexual Molestation

We might begin to think, then, that nothing could be worse for young girls than not having a father in the home. It turns out that the absent father may not be as damaging to his daughter's feelings of self-worth as is the presence of a sexually abusive father, stepfather, uncle, older brother, or mother's lover who lives in the home. The absence of a caring and responsible father figure goes beyond the psychological realm into the issue of the safety and security of the children in the home. Children without an adult male to protect them run a greater risk of sexual molestation. Two-thirds of the teen mothers in a 1992 study had been sexually abused or raped by a parent or other adult male. The offenders' mean age was 27.4 years.

Try to imagine the lingering effects on teens who have been sexually abused, who have experienced rape, or who have been forced into incestuous sex by a family member. If society has any questions about the importance of daughters having a supportive and sustaining relationship with their fathers, these stories should answer them.

> *Jenine, 16*: I never knew my real dad. Mom told me a little about him, but she was never married to him, and by the time I was born he was gone. I sat across a room from him once, but I decided I didn't want anything to do with him by then.

> Mom is married for the third time now, and I'm glad to have a good man in the house because my first stepfather abused me. He started when I was about 5 and never quit until he left the house when I was 11. I never said anything to my mom because I was so embarrassed and frightened by him.

At 14, when I got to be a teenager, and I had the normal problems of a kid that age, all the stuff that had gone on in those
years came back, and I freaked out. I ran away from home. I
stayed just anywhere or I stayed with friends. Anytime anyone touched me it triggered memories and I got freakier. I
thought I could run from it but of course I couldn't.

Rosalyn, 23: I want to forget the vision of my brother, plung-
ing, hurting. Emotions scarring me, ruining my spirit. It's like
larvae that gets inside you and eats you up from the inside
out. I want to ignore the world, pretend that castles and Prince
Charmings do exist, that love lasts, that feelings are true.

I was sexually abused by the babysitter's son when I was 7. My
brother raped me when I was 8. It colored my thinking about
men, and I've never felt secure about my relationships with
guys since then.

A Legacy of Molestation, Rape, and Incest

As fervently as we would wish that rape and incest were rare, the
National Women's Study of 4,000 women in 1992 learned that one-
eighth had been raped, a projected 12.1 million, two-thirds of them
before reaching 18, and one-third of these before they were 11. Most
survive, but their legacy is early parenthood, memory loss, poor self-
image, loss of childhood, a too-early adulthood, and painful memories of abuse.

Why would a young woman who had been sexually assaulted as a
young girl want to have sex at 13 or 14, or even older, I wondered. The
question haunted me. Wouldn't she be disgusted, turned off, frightened?

Two counselors at alternative high schools, one with twenty years
of experience, told me that although you'd think that a girl who'd
been sexually abused wouldn't want any part of sex, it seems to work
the other way. They don't feel they're good for much, but if somebody wanted them enough to force it on them, they must be good
enough for that. Their low self-esteem gets a boost if somebody pays
attention to them, expresses love or caring, and wants to have sex. So
they do, and many of them get pregnant.

Dr. Debra Boyer of the Women's Studies Program at the University of
Washington in Seattle agrees that the effects of sexual abuse in adolescence are linked to early sex. She writes that sexual abuse affects children in all areas of development. They are at higher risk for mental
health and social functioning problems than are non-molested children.

Victims see themselves as living in a world of unpredictable or
uncontrollable events, a world in which actions have no rational consequences. Such young women are at higher risk for adolescent pregnancy. Dr. Boyer's research found that 62 percent of the pregnant and

parenting teens she interviewed had been sexually molested or raped prior to their first pregnancy.

Older Men: Another Risk Factor

Male predators are another risk factor for young female teens. Because of their youth, inexperience, need for attention, and poor self-image, they may be vulnerable to adult male predators at rates that mock the notion that most teenage sex resulting in childbirth takes place between teenagers. Fifty percent of the fathers of babies born to teenage women are five or six years older than the mother. Two-thirds of these males are 20 years of age or older. Even more revealing is the statistic that the younger the teen, the older the male.

> *Fran, 18*: I lived alone with my mom. I met the baby's father at a concert last year, and I couldn't stand him. But when we began to go places and have fun, I liked him better. He was 24 when I was 17, and he had money. He was in college. One night he stayed at my house and we had sex. I got pregnant.

Fran fits the profile of the teen who is trapped and thinks the older male is a way out of her situation. Now she lives at home, another generation of single mother with her child. But this is not sexual molestation, you will say. No, it sounds more like a willingness on Fran's part.

The problem is that what a teenager sees as a way out (older male, some money, perhaps some education) turns into a one-night stand, which the father may forget and the mother lives with for the rest of her life.

Mothers Who Cannot Cope

We can't place all the blame for early teen sex on men. . . . Mothers of teens have a role, too. The teens talked about their mothers' alcoholism, physical abuse, drug abuse, prostitution, and—far less dramatic, but equally debilitating—just plain neglect.

> *Ginger, 13*: Mom's an alcoholic, so life with her was hard. During the week when she was working, things weren't too bad. But then the weekend would come, and she'd really let go with the drinking. Things were very bad then. She'd get verbally abusive and lose control of herself.

> I knew when I told her I was pregnant she'd hit the roof, and she did. She was fifteen when she first got pregnant and decided to have the baby adopted. When she got pregnant again she was 22 and thought she'd better get married. That ended in divorce when I was two. I really never saw my dad much then, except summers, and I haven't seen him recently, not since I was nine years old. . . .

Gail, 17: My sister and I lived with my mom, and we lived in lots of places. Finally we settled here, hoping things would be better. But Mom was still doing drugs and prostitution, and it didn't look like things would improve. I was into drugs, too, and I had missed a lot of school with that and all the moves.

One night, about a year after the move, we had a big argument. I wanted to go to school but she wanted me to stay home and help her after an operation she had. We fought about it and she went out, probably looking for guys and booze. My sister and I were hungry so we went out shopping for food.

We got home and were fixing something to eat when she came in drunk and started throwing the food around the kitchen. We couldn't help laughing at her because she looked so funny, and she got so mad that she threw us out. . . .

Irma, 16: When I was growing up my mom was wild. She had all different kinds of boyfriends and dragged us around to wherever she was going. My own father was not ready to settle down, she told me, and she wasn't ready to stay home and take care of us either. She's the kind who worries about herself and her current boyfriend, but doesn't worry about my sister or me.

Parenting Siblings

Another situation that has been both cited by researchers and recounted by teens has to do with too-early parenting of siblings. When single mothers who are not poor need to leave home, whether to work, to date, or to do errands, they hire a babysitter. When mothers living in poverty, even the working poor, need to leave home, they put their oldest child in charge of the younger ones. These babysitters, still children themselves, tell their stories:

Adrienne, 17: . . . When I lived with my mom, I wasn't really happy because I was only a kid myself, and I became the babysitter. I was scared about the job. And I wanted to go out and play, but I had to babysit. I wanted freedom, but my mom didn't understand that at all. She was studying to become a nurse, and she made it. Even though I know she had to do what she did, I resented it then, and I think I still do.

When the smaller kids finally got old enough to be left alone, I didn't even want to go out anymore. I had no friends to play with, and by then I had stopped asking her to let me go out, so I've never been to a football game or to a basketball game, and I only recently started to go out to movies. I went to one school dance, but I was scared and alone, and it wasn't any fun. So I'm not afraid of losing my freedom when my baby is born because I never had any anyhow.

Anne, 21: I wanted to go out and play with the other kids, but no, I had to stay home and babysit my brother again. I wouldn't have minded if I thought my parents really cared about me, too, but I knew they didn't because when they finally got home from work they never talked to me about anything except my brother. How was he? Did I take good care of him? I could have thrown something at all of them. . . .

When I was 12, I finally found someone who paid attention to me and expressed his love for me. We became lovers, and at 14 I had Robbie. I guess taking care of my brother helped me in some ways because I knew a lot about taking care of Robbie when he was born. I know how lonesome and unloved I felt, and I make sure this doesn't happen to my son.

Tammy, 14: When I was four my mom didn't take good care of us. She was on drugs, cocaine and crack, and she'd go out and never come home. I had two sisters younger than me, and I was taking care of them as best I could. I diapered them and tried to feed them. . . . I was the only supervision they had.

I knew my mom needed me, and I knew Grandma treated her awful. She fought with her. So did Mom's sister. She tried to run Mom over with a car, and I felt I had to help her. . . .

Being a mom myself at 14 isn't hard.

Shunika, 18: And where was Mom? Like Dad, she worked days and many nights to try to keep the family going in our small, poor, rural town. They really tried, I see now, but the problem for me was that I had a younger brother, and he needed to be cared for. So when I turned eight and he was five, I became his mom. I'm proud to say I did a good job for him—he's a good student, a good athlete, and best of all, he has self-esteem. He thinks he's great, and he is.

For me, though, I was too young to be taking care of a little boy. I needed a mom myself, and she just couldn't do it. . . .

Neither parent ever had—or made—the time for us, and I never heard anything good about myself. I was never told by either one of my parents that I was pretty, or smart, or would amount to much. So I fell for the first boy who came along and told me I was pretty and smart, and that's how I got pregnant at 17.

My parents were sure I would never amount to anything. You tend to believe your parents, and I guess I thought they had it right.

Adrienne, Anne, Tammy and Shunika were all fearful. They were deprived of their freedom when they were just learning how to use it. They wanted their own lives, but they were tied down to a responsibility they weren't ready for. They couldn't make friends of their own, the business of childhood, because they had to take on the business of adulthood, becoming acting mothers when they were still children. In adolescence, since mothering was how they were valued most, why not have their own babies? They were developed enough to conceive them.

It's too late to be a kid anymore, they realize, and they don't even know how to be. Might as well do what they know how to do. They were important in that role once; they could be again. . . .

The Single Mother as a Role Model

The research also tells us that teens whose mothers were single when they gave birth are more apt to become single mothers than other teens. The single mother is the only female role model the teen knows. Her mother was young. Why shouldn't she be? Her mother did it alone. Why can't she? Who needs a man to raise a child?

Candy, 18: I like being a mom. I always wanted to be a young mom. Mom was 16 when she had me. She understands me because she's young, and I want to be like that with my daughter.

I was 16 when I started having sex. He was 21. But that broke up fast, and I didn't have sex again until I met the father of my baby. He's 18, too, and he's a good guy. Our baby is 6 months old. I knew I could get pregnant, but I didn't worry about it because I really wanted to have a baby.

Mindy, 16: "Don't get pregnant at 16 like I did, Mindy." That's what my mom used to say to me from the time I was 13. She'd say it over and over, but she didn't say much else. In fact, she didn't talk to me at all. I was aching to talk to her about that and about other stuff that kids worry about, but she never had the time. Just time for "Don't get pregnant at 16 like I did, Mindy."

Why should I listen to her, I thought. She doesn't really care about me. So you know the story. I got pregnant at 15. When I was a kid I remember feeling pretty good about myself most of the time, but then something bad would happen and all the good feelings would be gone. That's how it is now.

Peer Pressure

And what role does peer pressure play? How many times have we, as parents, heard our children tell us that "everybody's doing it"? It turns out that peer pressure is more important for some teens than others. Being lonely and feeling neglected by the parent or parents who are at home leads many girls to try to find friendship and love "out there."

Jim Oliver, a social studies teacher at an alternative high school, having worked with adolescents for 30 years, tells us that the peer groups know how to pick out likely recruits. They spot the young teens who are needy. They have a knack for knowing who's looking for affiliation. They know which kids will resist the pressure and which kids won't. They reach out to the teens who need affirmation that they are attractive and worthwhile, and who, if they can't get it at home, will search for it in their peers.

The teens become part of a group, and follow the standards set by the crowd. If the crowd is drinking or doing drugs, they do it, too. If the group is having sex, they will, too. Oliver says that a strong, loving relationship with a parent is the best defense against peer pressure.

> *Jewel, 17*: My mom still thinks it was her, but it wasn't. It was me. I was a spoiled kid, and I wanted my own way. When I couldn't get it, I did whatever I needed to get it. So when things were awful at school, when the girls pushed me around, and when I started fighting with my mom over everything, I just left home.
>
> I was 14, kind of young, but I knew I had to get away from the fighting and I had to have control over my own life. I had some older girlfriends by then, kids 16 or so, and they were having sex, so I decided to have it, too.
>
> Then I moved in with my boyfriend. We both worked and that's how we could afford an apartment. I lived with him for two years, and I was taking the pill so I thought I couldn't get pregnant. But I did.
>
> *Josie, 17*: I had plenty of love when I was a kid. My parents were great. They blame themselves, but it's not their fault. I just got in with the wrong crowd. I got into sex much too early. We didn't do drugs or alcohol, but sex was the thing. . . .
>
> I made bad decisions. I decided to have sex and I didn't pro-

tect myself, so here I am pregnant and about to have a baby. I'm smart and I'm a good student, but I sure wasn't smart about this. . . .

Choosing to Get Pregnant

Some people say teens have babies because they want to. . . . While we can't determine their deepest motivations, we can listen to their words.

Sarah, 16: I chose to have a baby because my dad came home and wanted to take my twin sister and me to the North where he lived, and I thought if I got pregnant he wouldn't be able to take me.

He could, I guess, but he doesn't want to now because he thinks it's better for me to stay with my boyfriend. So I'm living with Mom. . . .

Shawn, 16: I wanted this child. I planned it. I was living with my dad, and I was lonely because he was drinking hard. My boyfriend told me he had been told he couldn't have children and he thought I'd leave him because of that. So I set out to prove to him that I wouldn't leave him, and I got pregnant.

I wanted this child for another reason, too. I wanted a child because it mattered to me to have someone to love the way I love her.

Rhonda, 17: I chose to get pregnant. I wanted a baby, so I slept with a guy. Two weeks later I changed my mind, but it was too late. I never considered adoption. I felt it was my responsibility to keep her. I'm glad I did because I love her very much. . . .

I wanted to get pregnant because I was so lonely. My mom worked and there was no one at home. After work she went to bars. So at 14 I found a man. I was sure he was "the one." He was my first love, the first man I ever slept with. Now that he's a dad he's a deadbeat. He never calls or visits, and he owes me child support.

. . . Most of the teens I interviewed told me they did not plan to become pregnant. Only three of the fifty said pregnancy was intentional.

According to *Sex and America's Teenagers,* 15 percent choose to have a child. This may be closer to the reality. Max Schilling, Teenage Parent Program Specialist for the Florida Department of Education in Tallahassee, feels that a lot of teens don't know for sure. They may have fleeting moments when they think it could work. They may fantasize about a beautiful baby to hold, to be needed and loved by, to love. While many may know their consensual sexual activities may result in pregnancy, they are ambivalent, so do not actively prevent conception. . . .

Some Other Factors

Still other factors, one societal and two developmental, are given by researchers and professionals focusing on adolescents:

- The fact that our society is laden with sexual symbols, in the media and in the real world as well, surely sets the tone, especially for poor teens who don't have opportunities to do other things to give them satisfaction.
- As we continue to make progress in science, medicine and nutrition, the age of onset of menarche continues to decrease, typically at age 12 in 1988 compared with age 15 in 1890.
- Learning disabled students, whose reading and writing skills are not sufficiently developed to be successful in school, are more apt to become teen mothers than are their academically successful peers. . . .

A Matter of Choice?

Are teens having sex earlier? Yes, they are. The age of first sex has decreased, according to all the studies. Among children born in the decade of the 30s, 43 percent of males and 32 percent of females had sex before age 18. By the 60s, 61 percent of males and 58 percent of females had sex before age 18, a 16 percent increase for males and a 26 percent increase for females.

Are more teens having babies? Kristin Moore, Child Trends, Inc., reports that despite a rise in the 80s, the teen birthrate is lower now than it was in the 60s. What is higher is the number of unmarried teens having babies. The reality is that while there are more children being born to single mothers, most of them are adults, not teens. Seven out of every ten single mother births are to women 20 years of age and older.

Are they choosing to have early sex, and are they choosing to have babies? In spite of the tendency to blame the victim, it's hard to blame a teenager who is sexually abused, perhaps raped by a member of the family, mother's boyfriend, a family friend, or an older stranger. In cases of early sexual abuse, followed by consensual teenage sex, the data tells us that these teens are far more likely than most to engage in early sex. Their self-esteem is diminished; they may feel worthless except for sex. When teens have sex with older men, they have either fallen victim to male predators, or in their immaturity and inexperience they have sought the security of a man who they think will take care of them and take them away from their environment. Not too much choice there, either.

But what of the teen who has consensual sex with another teen? This sounds more like choice though we, being adults, cannot know the full power of peer pressure and societal pressure to conform to the sexual mores of this decade.

What of the teen who says, "I wanted a child"? Surely there is a choice being made here. Yes, there are some who say this, and I think they mean it. But nearly every teen mother I spoke to—whether she said she got pregnant intentionally or not—felt she was much too young to be a mother and wished she had waited.

Second and third births to unmarried teens indicate that this may be the area in which real choice is made. However, a more likely alternative to this thinking is that the same factors that induced early sex and early pregnancy may still be at work with teens for whom there has been no successful intervention.

The Disturbing Consequences of Teen Pregnancy

Paul V. Trad

In the following selection, psychiatrist Paul V. Trad describes the ways in which pregnancy is especially traumatic for adolescents. Because teens are already undergoing significant developmental changes, he writes, they are less able to deal with the additional physical and psychological changes that accompany pregnancy. According to Trad, pregnancy upsets the ordinary process of a teen's physical growth, making it difficult for her to accept many of the changes that normally take place during puberty. He explains that teen pregnancy also can have wide-ranging psychological consequences which, when combined with the emotional changes of puberty, can seriously influence a pregnant teen's self-image, ability to cope, relationships with others, and feelings associated with the forthcoming child and motherhood. A former associate of the Cornell University Medical Center, the late Paul V. Trad authored numerous books on infant and adolescent mental health and developmental patterns. Prior to his death, he wrote the "Infant and Child Psychiatry" column for *Psychiatric Times*.

Researchers concur that pregnancy is a time of dramatic transition. A first-time pregnancy heralds a change from the status of woman to that of mother. The significance of this change is reflected in the terminology used to describe pregnancy; words such as "metamorphosis" and "transformation" are commonly applied. Some developmentalists have even referred to the pregnancy period as a time of crisis during which the woman undergoes not only psychological upheaval, but a revision of her sense of self and identity. While these changes are noteworthy for the adult woman confronting pregnancy, their effect is frequently magnified when the expectant mother is an adolescent.

Adolescent pregnancy is an issue that warrants the attention of developmentalists. The problem not only burdens individual teenagers and their newborn babies, but its widespread prevalence affects all strata of society and has begun to take a toll on welfare resources.

Excerpted from Paul V. Trad, "Assessing the Patterns That Prevent Teen Pregnancy," *Adolescence*, Spring 1999. Reprinted with permission from Libra Publishing, Inc.

Statistics help place the problem in perspective. Teenage pregnancy rates in the U.S. are at the highest level among Western nations. . . . However, the reasons are not fully understood. Some proposed explanations include lack of knowledge about birth control, cultural differences that place esteem on adolescent motherhood, the teenager's sense of insecurity or impulsivity, dependency needs, and attempts to assert independence.

Sexual activity among teenage girls has become, in many communities, the norm rather than the exception. . . . Teenagers are the least likely age group to practice contraception. Equally troubling is that the annual pregnancy rate among teenagers 14 years of age or younger continues to rise.

Teen Mothers Face Greater Dangers

Moreover, the adolescent mothers' problems intensify during the prenatal and antenatal periods. Specifically, prenatal medical care is frequently delayed or inadequately delivered. . . . According to a 1991 article in *Clinical Pediatrics,* among the complicating factors of teenage pregnancy is the high incidence of sexually transmitted diseases, which have been associated with an increased risk of preterm labor and low infant birth weight. A delay between verification of the pregnancy and first obstetric visit may also place the fetus at risk. . . . Low birth weight has been associated with increased levels of neonatal morbidity and mortality. Moreover, the low birth weight of infants born to adolescent mothers has been associated with unfavorable maternal health care factors, such as substance abuse, low income, single-parent status, and low educational level. According to E. Ringdahl, family physicians can help curtail the trend of rising teenage pregnancies by identifying adolescents likely to engage in sexual behavior and providing contraceptive counseling. Follow-up is also recommended since adolescents harbor the unrealistic perception that they are invulnerable to pregnancy and may therefore not use contraceptives on a regular basis.

In addition, the consequences of adolescent pregnancy may extend far beyond the birth. Pregnancy during the teenage years almost inevitably results in an interruption of the adolescent's education. Often, the teenager drops out of school. . . . Teenage mothers earn approximately half as much as their counterparts who are not adolescent mothers. Two-thirds of the children of teenage mothers live below the poverty level by the age of six years. . . .

Beyond the statistics, however, a host of other issues relate to the ability of the adolescent mother to endure the pregnancy successfully and to properly minister to the child after the birth. It is known, for example, that pregnancy is a time of emotional upheaval for the expectant mother, even under the most optimal conditions. Women undergo a full spectrum of physical and psychological changes at this time. . . . When the expectant mother is physically and psychologically mature, these experiences can be highly beneficial in preparing the woman for the responsibilities she will encounter with the infant. When the expectant mother is an adolescent, however, the dramatic shift in perspective that accompanies a normal pregnancy may become overwhelming. It should be remembered that the adolescent has not yet attained either physical or psychological maturity. With the onset of pregnancy, the teenager can no longer continue the normative strivings for identity that characterize the behavior of most of her peers. Instead, a kind of developmental arrest occurs and she is forced to focus on the pregnancy and its consequences. As a result, the pregnant teenager may engage in maladaptive behaviors and inappropriate emotions that affect not only her own development, but may influence her eventual relationship with the infant. . . .

Developmental and Physical Consequences

As a developmental phase, adolescence is positioned between childhood and adulthood. Most texts identify the onset of puberty as the end of childhood and the beginning of adolescence. As a result, the physical and sexual maturation associated with adolescence has always been a significant component of this developmental period. Equally important, however, are the psychological dimensions of adolescence. Conventional theory holds that adolescence is a time during which teenagers assert their sense of identity, rebelling from the control and authority of their parents. Thus, it is not unusual to encounter a high degree of emotional turmoil in the adolescent.

When a teenager becomes pregnant, however, the continuity of both the physical and the psychological growth is abruptly interrupted. The teenager's physical maturation begins to play a secondary role as the process of gestation comes to predominate. Moreover, unless the pregnancy represents an unconscious means of asserting autonomy, the teenager's opportunities to express her independence from her parents will meet with new constraints as the pregnancy progresses. One of these constraints involves the adolescent's rapid transformation into a parent herself. Needless to say, pregnancy, even under the most optimal circumstances, signifies a dramatic maturational change for the woman. When the pregnant woman is a teenager, the normal developmental upheaval caused by the gestation process will be superimposed upon the turbulence of adolescence. The result is often confusing, interfering with both the expectant mother's developmental course, as well as her ability to initiate a relationship with her unborn infant. . . .

Adolescents who become pregnant will experience two physical processes at once—the normally dramatic physical changes that occur during the teenage years and the radical hormonal changes triggered by the gestational process. Specifically, adolescence is a time of physical development culminating in the ability to engage in mature sexual activity. Most organ systems exhibit substantial growth during adolescence, with the most growth taking place in the reproductive system. Moreover, sexual maturity is achieved at an earlier age today than it did at the turn of the twentieth century. For example, the average age of menarche has decreased by approximately three months each decade until recently and is matched by a comparable precocity in the sexual development of boys. Young girls now experience menarche at an average age of 12.8 to 13.2, with a range of 10 to 16 years. This earlier onset of reproductive maturity means that adolescents will be prone to engage in sexual activity at earlier ages. . . .

It appears that most teenagers engage in sexual activity for experimental purposes, meaning that they are responding to urges to explore curiosities about bodily sensations. Beyond this exploratory interest, however, teenagers may also engage in sexual behavior to satisfy unfulfilled emotional needs. Moreover, adolescents whose lives lack structure may be at a heightened risk for sexual activity very early in their lives. A lack of structure may emerge in the form of less parental support, fewer parental controls, and less parental supervision over behaviors likely to culminate in sexual activity. Psychological problems have also been correlated with early and frequent sexual activity. Depression, drug abuse, and mothering difficulties have all been associated with early initiation of sexual behavior. Some investigations have suggested that depressed teenage women may rely on sexual gratification to achieve nonsexual goals. Specifically, these girls may use sex to feel loved and to establish intimacy with another individual.

In other respects, adolescent pregnancy disrupts the ordinary processes of physical growth. One vital aspect of sexual identity for an adolescent girl is the manner in which her body has changed. When a teenager becomes pregnant, however, her body rapidly changes once again. However, changes such as gaining weight may not attract the sexual attention of peers. The teenager's increased weight may preclude her from engaging in an active social life and from having sexual relations. These changes may have detrimental effects. By not allowing the teenager to grow accustomed to the normal changes of adolescence, pregnancy precludes exploring her individuality and ability to relate to other people. Adolescent pregnancy, then, may impede the teenager's adaptive understanding of her physical maturation.

Psychological Consequences

The psychological consequences of teenage pregnancy are wide ranging and diverse. As a maturational attainment, pregnancy causes radical changes in the personality and emotional characteristics of the pregnant adult woman. Indeed, A. Coleman and L. Coleman proposed that pregnancy may cause an altered state of consciousness during which the pregnant woman is preoccupied with fantasies and dreams as "omens" pertaining to the future, as well as the unborn infant.

These perceptions may be grossly exaggerated when the expectant mother is an adolescent and the pregnancy was unplanned. The emotional confusion that surfaces in the pregnant woman may also cause her to blur the boundaries between "self" and "other." As the infant develops within the mother's body, there tends to be a "merging" of identities on both a physical and psychological level. Resolution of this sense of merging will ultimately need to occur after the birth as the mother separates physically and emotionally from the infant. Most mentally healthy adult pregnant women are capable of withstanding this process, so that they can eventually relate to their infant in an adaptive manner. Because they have not yet achieved a full-fledged sense of their own identity, however, many adolescent mothers will be unable to experience this form of adaptive separation. Instead, pregnant adolescents tend to harbor poor or distorted mental concepts of the fetus. S.L. Hatcher, for instance, noted that pregnant teenagers envision the unborn infant as a nonobject, an "it." When asked to depict the fetus within them, these girls tend to draw unappealing, unrealistic images. Although pregnant girls in the middle years of adolescence entertain slightly more adaptive representations, they still draw the fetus as being grossly oversized, a depiction that corresponds to their fantasy of feeling overwhelmed by the baby. These images suggest that the adolescent is prey to serious misperceptions concerning the pregnancy and its meaning. Specifically, the adolescent may use the pregnancy to express her own unresolved dependency needs, to substitute for a lost nurturing parent, or to achieve a form of separation and independence from her parents. The results of this misconception can be manifold. The adolescent may fail to visit the obstetrician for regular visits or not follow instructions regarding diet, smoking, or alcohol consumption. After all, if the adolescent has a nonexistent or distorted image of the developing baby, she will probably be unable to predict that certain behaviors during the pregnancy will have known detrimental repercussions after the birth.

Pregnancy is also known as a time during which the woman's emotional responses become heightened. The dreams and fantasies of women confronting imminent motherhood are known to contain powerful mixtures of anxiety, fear, and/or depression. . . .

Expiating these strong emotions is often difficult for expectant teenagers. Pregnancy can overwhelm the teenager's burgeoning sense of control over her life. She may feel fear, shame, guilt, and anger. She may be afraid to tell her parents that she is pregnant and be angry at the infant's father. Above all, she will have to make an important decision shortly after the pregnancy is confirmed. Should she carry the baby to term or have an abortion? Both of these decisions awaken a sense of uncertainty. How will she respond emotionally if she has an abortion? Similarly, how will her life be altered if she carries the infant to term and decides to raise the child? Unfortunately, the teenage years are not a time when crucial decisions are readily resolved. . . .

Pregnancy interferes with the adolescent's need to assert independence from her parents. Generally, this is a gradual process that occurs over a period of years. As the adolescent asserts autonomy, she may experience a sense of accomplishment and pride. Through these cautious steps, psychological strength and mastery accumulate. But pregnancy can erase years of progress and psychological independence in a short period of time. Suddenly, the teenager is at the mercy of her body. She may be forced to rely on her mother or both parents to make decisions and to execute a plan of action. The adolescent and her parents become once again locked in a dependent relationship, as if a developmental regression has occurred.

In some instances, the adolescent uses the pregnancy to express childhood needs that have been unmet, to substitute for the loss of a nurturing parent or to accomplish a pseudo-separation from the parents. If used for these purposes, the teenager is at risk of failing to acknowledge the realities of motherhood. In these circumstances, both the mother and the infant will probably experience negative consequences. A mother who is unable to directly envision and predict the needs of the infant during the pregnancy will be apt to neglect or ignore them after the birth. From the mother's point of view, the pregnancy will be a frustrating, unfulfilling, and even destructive experience. The mother may begin to frame negative expectations of the future. She may view the pregnancy as interfering with her own independence, resent the increasing demands the infant makes upon her body, and eventually resent the infant as an object that has seriously restricted her independence.

These negative expectations are often overwhelming. Adolescents may be torn between resenting the limitations the pregnancy has placed upon their activities and feeling guilty and responsible for the pregnancy. These emotions are likely to escalate as the delivery approaches, especially if the pregnancy has been unplanned or is unwanted. Frequently, the expectant adolescent becomes mistrustful of relationships with men. In this regard, she may note that the infant's father changed his attitude as soon as he became aware of the pregnancy. Moreover, adolescent mothers rarely marry the presumed father of the child who is generally also a teenager. It is not difficult to understand how the teenage girl may begin to feel cheated. She can no longer lead the carefree life associated with adolescence. Now she has responsibilities and, in any event, her rapidly altering physical state is an impediment. In addition, it is probable that her education has been interrupted and that her chance for socioeconomic security has been marred or at least deferred. Even if she marries the infant's father, her prospects for the future remain bleak, since teenage marriages are several times more likely to end in divorce as compared to those between more mature persons.

A Real Live Baby

The young girl who carries the infant to term is ultimately confronted with the reality of caring for a real live baby. This responsibility may be overwhelming and preclude her from establishing her own identity. Unlike other teenagers, the young adolescent mother will not have time to devote to her own concerns. Her days will be spent meeting the demands of the infant. In these circumstances, it is not unusual for many adolescent mothers to resent their own babies. The adolescent may have anticipated that the infant would show her affection in a way others in her life have not, with an adoring and unconditional love. But the reality of having a newborn baby may be quite different. Infants are dependent creatures, an outcome many adolescents have not anticipated. This quality may be strongly resented by the adolescent mother who may feel that her own needs are rarely, if ever, gratified immediately. Resentment, in turn, may cause the mother to fail to respond adaptively to the infant.

An equally dismal scenario may occur when the girl becomes pregnant as a distorted effort to separate from her mother and assert her own independence. Such an adolescent may perpetuate a cycle of dependency that is grounded in resentment toward the person she depended on—in this case, her mother—as well as resentment transposed onto the infant, who has begun to infringe upon the adolescent mother's independence. The teenage mother will be hard-pressed to help her infant achieve independence when she feels that she has been deprived of this very achievement. While mature adult mothers possess the psychological maturity to sublimate their own needs to those of the child, for adolescent mothers this skill is more difficult.

Another issue that may be especially poignant for adolescent expectant mothers involves resolving discrepancies between the "fantasy" baby envisioned during the pregnancy and the "real" baby when it is born. . . . The real baby may not look exactly as the mother had envisioned, or behave as she had anticipated. The real baby may not respond to the mother, and she may suddenly feel that the infant is a stranger. The risk of experiencing this disappointment after the birth is heightened if the "real" baby differs a great deal from the adolescent's preconceived notions of the "fantasy" baby, while much initial pleasure may be derived from a "real" baby who closely mirrors the expectations of the "fantasy" baby. . . .

While mature mothers are able to "grieve" the loss of the fantasy child, but fairly rapidly adjust to an acceptance of the real infant, adolescent mothers have greater difficulty with this process. One reason may be that as teenagers, they have not completed their own psychological growth and are therefore not as prepared to confront developmental change as are adult mothers. Suddenly, when the child is born, the irrevocable nature of the birth becomes a reality that cannot be avoided, but the adolescent cannot deal with this momentous change in her life.

COMMON TEEN REACTIONS TO BECOMING PREGNANT

Robert W. Buckingham and Mary P. Derby

Robert W. Buckingham is a professor of public health at New Mexico State University in Las Cruces and the author of numerous books. Mary P. Derby is a maternal child health clinical nurse specialist at Harvard Pilgrim Health Care in Boston, Massachusetts. The following selection is taken from their book *"I'm Pregnant, Now What Do I Do?"* Most teen pregnancies, the authors explain, are unintentional, creating intense emotional reactions in teens who became pregnant when they did not want—or expect—to. Buckingham and Derby write that feelings such as shock, anger, and guilt are common responses to unintentional pregnancies and can be overcome. According to the authors, many teens also go into denial. In their view, denial is a normal defense mechanism and is harmless so long as the teen does not stay in denial throughout the entire pregnancy.

Sara sat alone in her bedroom crying. Her period was almost two months late. Each morning for the past several days she had felt nauseated, and at times she had been sick to her stomach. Her breasts ached. The home pregnancy test she held taken that morning was positive. Sara was in shock, and wondered how this could have happened to her; at her age. She thought back to the one time she had had sex with her boyfriend, Andy. It had been his first time, too. How did she get pregnant the first time she'd had sex? No one could possibly be so unlucky, she thought. She was sure the pregnancy test must be wrong, but then she remembered that they hadn't used birth control. It had been the end of the summer: Andy was leaving for college. They were celebrating. They were both nervous, and got caught up in the moment. She didn't want to bring up birth control. They were having a special time. She didn't want to ruin it. Besides she had wanted to show him that she was mature, and just as grown-up as the college women she knew he would be meeting soon. Now I'm pregnant, sobbed Sara. How could I have let this happen? How could I have been so stupid? What am I supposed to do now? My life is ruined.

Sara didn't know who to turn to. Normally she would turn to her mom when she needed help; they had a good relationship. She struggled with whether she should turn to her mom now. She felt ashamed and guilty, and she worried about telling her mom. Her mother was going through a divorce, and the last thing Sara wanted to do was burden her mom with her pregnancy. She didn't want to add to the stress. Sara was afraid that the news of her pregnancy would destroy her mother. Sara thought about talking to one of her friends. Who could she trust? Her boyfriend Andy was a freshman in college. She was a sophomore in high school. Her friends didn't like Andy; they thought he was too old for her. She wasn't sure how he would react. She was afraid their relationship would end, and then what would she do? She wondered if Andy would want to be a father now, or would he abandon her?

Sara is not alone. Lots of teens become pregnant the first time they have sex because they do not use birth control. About 20 percent of all teens who become pregnant do so within one month of the first time they had sexual intercourse. Many of these teens react just like Sara did. They are angry, confused, and in shock. They are overwhelmed with their feelings. They're not sure whom they should talk to or whom they can trust. . . .

Why Teens Become Pregnant

Other teens become pregnant because they don't know how a pregnancy happens. There are a lot of misconceptions among teens about how to prevent a pregnancy. Some teens mistakenly believe that you can't get pregnant if you have sex standing up, if you have sex when you're very young or haven't gotten your period yet, or if you douche after you have sex. Some are willing to trust their boyfriend that he will withdraw or "pull out" on time. Jill says: "That's what I did. He told me, 'Don't worry, honey, it will be perfectly all right.' Well it wasn't. I got pregnant that night." Others take risks and think they will be okay because they're certain that they've calculated their "safe days," and think they are avoiding sex on days they believe they are fertile. This is an unreliable method. If this happened to you, there's no reason to feel stupid. Other teens have similar misconceptions and become pregnant when they don't want to.

Still other teens don't use contraception because they mistakenly believe they don't need to. They were lucky and didn't get pregnant the first time, so they took more chances, thinking that "it couldn't happen to them.". . .

About 50 percent of all teens who become pregnant for the first time become pregnant within six months of their first sexual experience. Many teens feel pressure to have sex. They think all their friends are sexually active, or they want to experiment and find out what it's all about. Unfortunately many begin sexual activity not fully understanding the responsibility and consequences of such activity. Many are shocked when they find they are pregnant when they didn't intend to become pregnant. They are faced with making a very difficult decision at a time in their lives when they don't feel prepared to.

There are other teens who do use birth control, at least some of the time. According to the Alan Guttmacher Institute, two-thirds of teens use some form of birth control, usually the male condom, the first time they have sexual intercourse. Sometimes teens make an attempt to use birth control, but they don't use it consistently and correctly every time they have sexual intercourse. Many teens don't anticipate having sex, so they don't prepare themselves. Many teens mistakenly believe that if you prepare yourself it's less romantic and less spontaneous. . . .

When these teens do become pregnant, they are as shocked and disappointed with themselves as young women are who don't use birth control. They feel very bad about getting pregnant and are hard on themselves. Carolyn became pregnant at age sixteen. She had been taking the pill for about a year, but Carolyn said:

> I kept forgetting to take my pills. I knew I was supposed to use back-up protection, but I didn't bother. I was preoccupied with our relationship. My boyfriend, Dave, had just received a football scholarship from a college on the West Coast. I knew it would be hard for us to get together and I was worried that our relationship wouldn't last. . . . I cried and cried when the nurse told me I was pregnant. I couldn't believe that I had let this happen. I had been on the pill for about a year, and until I was preoccupied about Dave leaving, I was always responsible about taking it. I felt good about that. But when I found out I was pregnant, I was devastated. I thought I had been so stupid to have forgotten to take my pills. I could have prevented the pregnancy. I blamed myself. I should have known better.

Most Teen Pregnancies Are Unintended

Some young women wanted to become pregnant. Sometimes a young woman makes the conscious choice to become pregnant, and sometimes it's an unconscious choice. Some teens want a baby so that they will have "someone to love" (and someone to love them); other teens want to begin motherhood at an early age. Maria says, "I'm seventeen. I just got pregnant. I'll be graduating from high school in a few months. My boyfriend will be, too. We're planning on getting married. I'm ready to be a mother. This is what I planned."

Other teens want to prove their independence to their parents. . . . Other teens are angry at their parents, and use sex as a way of getting revenge. Wendy says, "My parents are so uptight. They're always trying to control what I do. I hate it. It was almost worth getting pregnant, just to see the expressions on their faces."

The vast majority of teens who become pregnant say they did not intend to. Almost all teens feel devastated about their pregnancies, and many young women describe feeling numb, in shock, and having difficulty believing what has happened to them. They describe emotions such as feeling ashamed, guilty, stupid, and sad. They feel alone. These feelings are all normal. Becoming pregnant at a young age when you didn't intend to is a very scary thing to happen. . . . It's likely that you're feeling bad about yourself and about your pregnancy. You may wish you had done something differently. You may feel ashamed. You may be worried about telling your parents, your guardian, and/or your boyfriend. You may be feeling anxious, not sure how they will react. You may fear that your life is forever ruined, that your life has now changed in a way that you're not so sure you will like.

You may find these emotions overwhelming. It may be hard for you to feel good about yourself right now. These feelings are all normal. There's a lot to think about now. There are a lot of decisions to make. A lot of young women don't feel good about themselves when this happens to them. . . .

Sometimes an experience like an unintended pregnancy happens in our lives and causes us pain. At these times we can be very hard on ourselves. It's common to feel bad about ourselves, to feel we let ourselves down, to feel we let our parents down, or we let someone else close to us down. We wonder why we didn't do something differently. We second-guess ourselves. We're filled with self-doubts. Suddenly we don't feel capable of doing anything right. This can happen whenever we experience anything unexpectedly, such as an unintended pregnancy. Sometimes we feel our situation is worse because it seems like everything is going wrong all at the same time. For instance, you're fighting with your parents, you fail an important test in school, you come in second in a track meet, you break up with your boyfriend, you have a fight with your best friend, there is a death in your family, or your parents split up. These are stressful experiences. When they happen at the same time you're faced with an unintended pregnancy, it makes each experience seem even more overwhelming. Many teens worry that their life is doomed. This experience will change your life. You will hurt. You will experience a loss and feel pain. You will grieve for a while. And it's normal to have these feelings. It's part of life. . . .

Shock, Denial, Anger, and Guilt

Becoming pregnant at a young age is a crisis for many women. When a crisis happens in our lives, there are typical ways we respond and react. Some of these responses are shock, denial, anger, and guilt. . . .

The first response typically felt is shock. . . . Your body feels numb.

You're having difficulty absorbing what has happened. Like Sara, you may want to be by yourself for a while. You may find it difficult to talk to anyone else about what has happened. You may not have friends you think you can trust. Like Sara, you may be experiencing some difficulty at home and not want to talk to your parents. Courtney shares her experience. This is how she felt:

> I felt miserable. . . . I felt alone, afraid, and overwhelmed. I was probably in shock. I was on automatic pilot. My actions were robotlike. I went to work and went to classes. I did everything that I would normally do. . . . I was a very private person. . . . I found it tremendously difficult to discuss my situation with anyone other than Steve [the baby's father]. Don't get me wrong, Steve and I were not emotionally intimate, then or ever. We never had a meaningful or mature discussion about the pregnancy or our feelings for each other. However, there was no one else I could turn to. I wasn't close to my family, so I didn't feel I could turn to my parents or any of my brothers and sisters for support. I was also hesitant to turn to my friends.

. . . The next response many young women have is denial. You may experience this. You may be having a hard time comprehending intellectually what has happened to you. Sara described how she felt after she found out she was pregnant. She knew the pregnancy test she took was positive, yet she still had trouble believing that she was really pregnant. A little denial at first is normal. It's a defense mechanism. It cushions and protects you from the shock of your experience. It may help you to regroup and get some of your strength and energy back so you can begin your decision-making process. Some young women stay in denial throughout the entire pregnancy. This, of course, is not normal, and it's not good for you. If you plan on continuing your pregnancy, it can have negative consequences for both you and your baby. Every day you spend in denial you limit the choices that you have. . . .

There are a lot of reasons why some young women deny their pregnancy. Sometimes they don't recognize pregnancy symptoms and so they don't realize that they are pregnant. Sometimes they are so fearful of how their families will respond to their pregnancies that they hide their pregnancies. With each passing day that they are able to hide their pregnancy, they begin to really believe that they are not pregnant. This can last a short time, or it can last the entire pregnancy. This is not a healthy way to respond to your pregnancy for you or for your baby.

Theresa became pregnant at age fourteen and didn't realize she was pregnant until she went into labor. It was a frightening experience for her. She says:

I never realized I was pregnant. I remember having sex once with this guy. It was a stupid thing to do, so I blocked the entire experience out of my mind. My periods were always irregular. I was glad I had stopped getting them. I thought I had just gained some more weight. I was always on the heavy side. I never suspected I was pregnant. One night I started having really bad cramps. My mother brought me to the emergency room. After examining me, they knew I was pregnant. I delivered my baby about ten hours later. Everything happened so fast. It was so scary. I didn't have time to think about what was happening to me. I didn't have time to prepare myself. All of a sudden I was fourteen, and I had a baby to care for.

. . . Anger is another common response which many young women feel. Many young women wonder "Why me, why now? Why is this happening?" Anger is a normal and healthy response. You may be angry with yourself, and wish you had taken more precautions. You may be angry with your boyfriend, perhaps you feel he should have been more responsible, or perhaps he wants you to choose an option which goes against what you want to do. You may also be angry because right now you are forced to make a decision. Your pregnancy will not go away on its own. You will have to make a decision, and no one can make it for you. . . .

Monica became pregnant with her second child when she was twenty. Monica was experiencing other difficulties in her life at the time. She voluntarily gave custody of her first child to her parents so the child could be well cared for while Monica tended to her own needs. Monica was not happy about her second pregnancy, and was angry at herself for getting pregnant. She explains:

I was very disappointed in myself for getting pregnant. I felt stupid, like I should have known better. I was supposed to be getting my life together, and instead I got pregnant. I was very angry with myself. I kept thinking, why now? Why did I let this happen? I should have known better. I was distraught. I felt very vulnerable. My emotions were all over the place.

. . . Almost all the young women who shared their experiences felt some form of guilt about their pregnancy. Many felt they had done something wrong. Many felt they had hurt and disappointed their families, and felt bad about that. Sherrie felt particularly guilty about her pregnancy. She found out that she was pregnant at the end of her senior year in high school. She had plans to go away to college. Her mother and her father both worked two jobs to be able to send her to college. They didn't have college degrees, but they wanted their daughter to have a chance in life that they didn't have. Sherrie explains:

I was quite sad for some time. I was depressed and felt very bad about my pregnancy. Both of my parents had two jobs. They worked very hard and were saving all their money so that I could go to college. They never had that chance. They wanted so much for me to succeed. For years they had willingly made sacrifices, knowing that I would have an opportunity for a better life. I felt very guilty about my pregnancy. I felt I had let my patents down and they had such high expectations for me.

. . . Every woman who is pregnant is afraid and feels overwhelmed at times. When you're young, these feelings can be even stronger. Many of the young women who shared their experiences described feeling stupid and ashamed. . . .

Most Teens Continue Their Pregnancy

Teenage pregnancy is not something new. Over the years, many young women have gotten pregnant when they didn't intend to. . . . Each year as many as one million teens become pregnant. The vast majority of these teens say they never intended to get pregnant. According to the Alan Guttmacher Institute, about half of all pregnant teens will choose to continue their pregnancies, slightly over one-third will choose to terminate their pregnancies, and the rest will end in miscarriage. Only a few pregnant teens will choose to place their babies for adoption.

THE SOCIOLOGICAL ISSUES OF BLACK TEENAGE MOTHERHOOD

Elaine Bell Kaplan

Elaine Bell Kaplan is an assistant professor of sociology at the University of Southern California in Los Angeles. In the following selection from her book *Not Our Kind of Girl: Unraveling the Myths of Black Teenage Motherhood,* Kaplan presents the story of a black teenage mother named Susan. Kaplan describes Susan's school and family problems, including her love-hate relationship with her parents and her feelings about the uncle who sexually molested her for four years. The author offers insights on the reasons why Susan lacks effective strategies to handle the complexities of growing up in a stressful urban environment. According to Kaplan, Susan's story is prototypical in the urban African American community. Black teenagers are also at greater risk for teen pregnancy because they become physically mature earlier than other teenagers and have little or no access to accurate information about their sexuality, Kaplan contends.

In the East Oakland, California, neighborhood where sixteen-year-old Susan Carter lived with her two-month-old baby, her mother, and two sisters, there were no parks. Nor were there many supermarkets or movie theaters. Susan hung out with her friends at the East Oakland mall, a run-down shopping center peppered with fast-food stores, small clothing boutiques filled with trendy but inexpensive clothes, a Payless shoe store, and a popular video game arcade. Susan's family shared a small, neatly furnished two-bedroom apartment across the street from the mall. After the baby was born, Susan applied for Aid for Dependent Children (AFDC), but her application was turned down when the welfare worker informed her that her mother's $1,100 monthly salary as a nursing assistant exceeded the maximum allowed families of four.

Tall and pretty, with large, almond-shaped eyes that flashed when she smiled, Susan was a curious mix of adolescent and adult. . . . Often we talked as Susan pushed curly-haired Jarmella in her stroller

Excerpted from Elaine Bell Kaplan, *Not Our Kind of Girl: Unraveling the Myths of Black Teenage Motherhood.* Reprinted with permission from the University of California Press and the author.

as we walked around the neighborhood of tiny box-shaped single-family homes interrupted occasionally by three-story apartment buildings like Susan's. . . .

School and Family Problems

Susan's story was hardly unique. Nor was the path that brought her to this place, the path she described as "coping with tough times.". . .

School was "great" until the seventh grade, when Susan's classes became "boring and too easy," the teachers dull and uninspiring, and the work tedious. School was neither stimulating nor relevant. . . .

Susan did not get along with her teachers. Talking with her friends was easier than studying for classes. She began cutting classes to spend her days at the park with her friends talking about "this and that," and her school attendance "went downhill from there.". . . By the end of the ninth grade, she was flunking most of her classes. "I didn't care." Her voice sounded convincing, but the "I don't care" attitude seemed like a front, hiding deep anxieties about herself and her ability to do well in school.

Eventually Susan became passive and invisible when she was in the classroom. "I had to get out of school, just anything, to get out of school, something else besides school.". . . Finally, two months after she learned she was pregnant, she dropped out of school—at the very age when school should have been a priority in her life. . . .

When I asked Susan to talk about her personal life, she groaned. A sullen expression appeared on her moon-shaped face as she began to talk about her family. She was extremely angry at her mother. There had always been tension between them, and the hostility increased when Susan's mother realized she was expected to support her grandchild. Janet Carter, Susan's mother, had her own set of problems. Since he left, when Susan was young, Susan's father refused to pay child support and seldom visited the children. To make matters worse, Susan said, Janet Carter was experiencing problems at work. . . .

Susan was sympathetic with her mother, who worked "like a dog," but she was also concerned because her mother's salary barely supported the family. . . . Susan's sympathy, however, only went so far. She believed her mother was not living up to her responsibility to love and support her daughter no matter what happened to her.

She blamed her mother for everything that had happened to her since her father had moved out. Until a few months before Susan became pregnant, her father occasionally visited the family or called his daughters to chat. Susan liked being with him. She recalled that when she stayed with him the summer she turned thirteen, he turned every occasion, like the nightly cookouts on the backyard grill, into a major event. That summer he found her a job typing letters and working on the computer at the local library. She was thrilled. On the next visit, everything changed:

We just didn't get along at all. I just was going out and getting drunk and I'd come home and I'd say everything to him. You know, all the things he did to my momma and all the things I hated him for when I was younger. 'Cause you know, he really hurt my momma a lot. I told him I hated him. I told him everything he deserved, and he didn't like me after that.

He did not like Susan's criticism one bit. He took her home and told her mother that he could not handle her. She could put Susan in a foster home for all he cared. She did not hear from him again until a year later, when she was eight months pregnant.

He called and, ah, I mean my aunt got a hold of him. And I told him I was pregnant. He was pretty shocked. And the only thing he said was, "Well, I guess I really need to talk to you." And he said he was thinking about coming down in two weeks, down to the Bay area. And, ah, he told me he'd call me back later on that night. And he, ah (*nervous voice*), never did. I never heard from him after that. . . .

I think if my mother had stayed with my father and they would have talked to me and done a lot of things differently, I think I never would have gotten pregnant. I know I wouldn't have. . . .

She felt her father's strong authority as head of the house would have been enough to save her from getting pregnant. Because her father was absent from her life, she had no one to hold responsible for the way it was turning out. . . .

Victims of Sexual Abuse

Susan was four years old when her uncle, who often baby-sat her, began sexually molesting her and his own three-year-old daughter. "He did it to me and my cousin Rachel." The molestation continued for four years:

And that's one thing I'll never understand my mom. She knew that he did that to me. My whole family knows, and he still lives with my grandmother, and he's still in the family. She doesn't pay attention. . . . In fact, she doesn't even like me any more, because . . . I don't know . . . I guess she thinks . . . I hate it. And my mom still lets him come over here just to fix the car. I tell her, "Mom, I don't want him over here." And she says, "Well, Susan, he's got to fix my car." You know, her car comes first. . . .

—*Do you think that there may be a connection between the molestation by your uncle and your early pregnancy?*

> I don't know if that had anything to do with it. I know that
> after that I blocked it out. I know he was wrong. It just made
> me mad and I blocked it away. I just never wanted to think
> about it anymore. It didn't bother me after awhile.

That is, she was not bothered until she began to have recurring
dreams that stirred up her memories of the sexual abuse:

> You know the Freddy dude from the movie *Nightmare on Elm
> Street*? I had a bad nightmare about him. There was this same
> house that my uncle molested us in. And Freddy had us
> locked up there. When I woke up, I was crying. I was shaking.
> And I jumped in bed with my sister. This was not long ago.
> Before I got pregnant, I guess. I was suppose to see a psychol-
> ogist. It was all blocked up and it had to come out sometime.
> Those feelings are still there.

Susan's story of early childhood sexual abuse reveals a complex issue
that does not lend itself to simple explanations. Some evidence suggests
a connection between premature and harmful sexual experiences and
teenage pregnancy. A study of 445 Black teenage mothers reports that
more than 60 percent of them were forced to have an unwanted sexual
experience at some time in their lives; one-third were younger than
twelve at the time of the first forced experience. More than one-quarter
reported that they were harassed by family members.

Although the study does not directly link sexual abuse and teenage
pregnancy, it does suggest that sexual abuse may make young girls
feel tremendously vulnerable and dependent. . . .

I asked other teen mothers questions about sexual abuse. Some
said, "Absolutely not!" A few were vague: something may have happened, but they could not remember the details. Only twenty-six-
year-old Tonya Banks, a stout and intense older teen mother, recalled
being sexually abused by her uncle when she was eight years old.

Many teen parent counselors at the Alternative Center, where I
worked as a consultant, admitted hearing "a million stories" about
sexual abuse. Some counselors believed these "stories" to be true; others were leery. . . .

Learning About Sexuality

Often during my visits with Susan, we would walk over to McDonald's
to buy French fries, Susan's favorite food. Several times a group of
neighborhood teenage boys, lounging in front of the restaurant
jostling with each other and slapping high fives, yelled, "I'm gonna git
me some of that," when we walked past them. Susan would stare at
the ground. One day a group of boys began jokingly to describe various sexual acts they wanted to perform on Susan. We made a hasty
retreat. Susan was unnerved by the sexual harassment.

In her book *Black Macho and the Myth of the Super Woman*, Michele

Wallace describes the way men notice the physical development of a young girl such as Susan: "Some of the nice little old men who used to pat her on the head when she was a child begin to want to pat her on the ass when she is thirteen. The neighborhood pimps and hustlers begin to proposition her." Wallace contends that young girls (like Susan) are extremely vulnerable and are unprepared for the way men respond to their maturing bodies.

Susan was typical of the other teenagers in this study in that she developed physical maturity early. The Black teenage participants of one study developed early signs of pubertal changes by age nine, with menarche coming at 12.5 years of age on the average. By the time they reached the age of thirteen or fourteen, these girls found themselves confronting teenage boys' sexual advances earlier than White girls.

While Black teenagers may physically mature earlier than other teenagers, all teenagers are maturing faster than the women of their mothers' generation. . . . Girls today reach menarche, the time when they become capable of conception and sexual activity, as early as ten years old. . . .

Missing from Susan's talk about sexuality was a well-defined attitude about her sexuality or about abortion: "We just didn't worry about that stuff. We never thought about it—getting pregnant, really getting pregnant." The myth that they could not get pregnant during their first sexual intercourse was very popular among the teen mothers.

The idea that teenagers do not understand their reproductive abilities may surprise some, but it is that very lack of knowledge—part of a general belief system holding that young girls do not need to know about their bodies—that rendered Susan and the other teen mothers largely ignorant about their sexuality: "I didn't really know nothin' about douching or about birth control."

Susan did not remember who told her about sex and sexuality, but she was sure it was not her mother: "My mother didn't tell me about menstruation until I had my period, and I almost died. Never! She didn't even wanna talk about it. My mother, she wouldn't talk to me to really let me know what this was." Most of the teenage mothers did not fully understand the menstrual cycle. Most did not acknowledge their first menstruation, although it signaled a major change in their lives. They did not make the connection between the start of menstruation and their ability to become pregnant.

Nor did they discuss sexuality with their parents. Girls who did talk with their parents discussed dating and boyfriends but not sexual intercourse, morality, or birth control. . . .

Some of the teen mothers admitted they were curious about sex. Several tried to talk to their parents. Sixteen-year-old Marnie Martin recalled being a little frightened by her feelings and wanting to talk to her parents, but, "That was the problem! My parents didn't really talk to me about sex. They used to say that 'you couldn't really have sex.'"

Marnie did find the courage to talk to her mother:

> I think I was thirteen when I first started having sex. My best
> friend thought I was crazy, 'cause I went to my mother and
> said, "Well mom, I like this boy and I might be doing some-
> thing with him and would you take me to get birth control?"
> And she said, "No, because once you start taking those pills
> you'll become sterile." See, I want kids. I love them and I
> want them. So it scared me. At the time the only thing I knew
> was condoms. I said no, I'm not going to mess with that.

. . . Four teen mothers told me that their mothers fell back on what
they had learned incorrectly from their own mothers. Tracy Alexan-
der laughingly mimicked her mother's high-pitched voice: "You can
get pregnant by kissing a boy." In a study on Black teenage mothers,
Joyce Ladner has found that mothers pass on to their daughters the
misinformation about sex and biological changes that their mothers
had passed on to them. . . .

The parents of many of these teen mothers believed that telling
their daughters about birth control could be interpreted as permitting
them to have sex. Several of the teen mothers' mothers admitted that
they did not know what to say to their daughters or how to be open
and frank about sexuality. . . .

"Everyone Is Doing It"

Susan met [her baby's father] Joney Glover, a "cute" seventeen-year-
old unemployed high school dropout, at a friend's party. He paid
Susan a great deal of attention at the party, which she found very
flattering. After that, they went everywhere together. Most of the
teen mothers had similar stories—meeting the babies' fathers at parties or at school, where boys hung around the school yard. When an
attractive girl crossed a boy's path, he gravitated to her very quickly,
arranged for a meeting, and encouraged a friendship that became
sexual in a short time. The "sexual hits"—the young mens' pickup
strategies—pervaded these teenage mothers' stories. When the girls
reached the ages of twelve and thirteen, they found the boys at school
talking to them, walking them home, and telling them how cute they
looked in whatever they wore.

Elizah Anderson argues that unprotected teenagers such as Susan
from mother-only households, or those who do not have a strong
male presence in the household, may be attracted to young men
eagerly selling themselves as ready for commitment. When I raised
this point with Susan, she quickly assured me that Joney had not
pressured her into sexual involvement. Joney was, after all, an ordinary boy in Susan's eyes. But according to Anderson ordinary boys
may be acting within a social context that allows them to develop the
kind of sexual harassment that writer Michele Wallace recalls. The

social context within which Black boys' sexual skills are developed consists of poverty, poor educational facilities, high unemployment, fatalistic attitudes, and the need to "prove" oneself through early sexual experimentation. The boys' attitude toward these girls is also consistent with the patriarchal view of women as sexual objects.

Susan did not know how racism and sexism might affect Black men like Joney. All she knew was that when she turned thirteen her mother allowed her to stay out later than before. Her friends pressured her to drink, smoke pot, and have sex. "Everyone is doing it," they informed her. "So I had to go with the crowd, that's what it was." Joney began to pay attention to her: "He was coming to school all the time to meet me." She was "scared." She did not have the time to think through her feelings about sexuality, dating, or birth control: "When be asked me, I didn't know what to do. But I did it finally."

Susan "did it," but sex did not have the erotic meaning usually associated with it: "It was disappointing. I regretted it afterward. I thought, God, is that all it is?". . .

We adults often perceive the world of adolescents through our own steamy glasses. Sometimes, rather than wanting to have sexual relations, teenage girls may simply want to be kissed and caressed. According to Robert Cole and Geoffrey Stokes, teenagers differ from adults in their reasons for engaging in sexual activity: for teenagers like Susan (and perhaps Joney), sex may be a reprieve from "a life that can be, often enough, boring or demanding or puzzling."

Cole and Stokes's observations made sense to me as I listened to Susan. In Susan's story I heard no words of hot desire or unbridled lust. Sex was a mechanical act, a way to release pent-up anxieties and tensions, as Cole and Stokes suggest, and perhaps an escape from her personal problems. . . .

We have to understand that Susan did not think it was morally wrong to engage in sexual intercourse. Like many teenagers, Susan valued the spontaneity and romance of her relationship with Joney, which would have been compromised by planning for sex. Several teen mothers thought that having sex before marriage was a "sin" but admitted overcoming that belief when they fell in love, echoing Susan's comment: "For the first time, I was really in love. So we had sex."

A Lack of Sex Education

"Why didn't you use birth control?" I asked Susan. Despite Leon Dash's observation that the teenage mothers in his study were knowledgeable about contraception, Susan did not learn about birth control from her mother or anyone else. Several teen mothers I spoke with made the same claim as those in Dash's study, but in fact few knew about birth control or other issues regarding their sexuality. For example, none of the teen mothers could adequately discuss the man's role in reproduction. Only two were well informed about contraceptives.

The use of contraceptives presents a dilemma to teenage girls. According to Kristen Luker, for the teenager to use contraceptives is an admission she is sexually active. If the teenage girl uses contraceptives, she loses all claim to spontaneity. If she buys contraceptives in the drugstore, she acknowledges in a fairly public place that she intends to have sex. Another part of the problem for teenagers is their ambivalence about norms governing their sexual behavior. Whose norms to follow—their peer group's or their parents'? How can they understand these norms, given that parents refuse to discuss them, other than to say, "You can't"?

"Why didn't you take sex education classes in school?" I asked Susan. She wanted to take a course on sex education, she told me, but the school did not offer one. A few teen mothers said their schools did offer these classes, but they were not very helpful. Two teen mothers who attended their schools' sex education programs found them to be too clinical, the language too technical, the teacher too aloof, and the material too removed from their real experiences. In most cases these classes were held only one day during the semester. . . .

The media also bear responsibility for poor sex education. According to Millicent Philliber, whose study criticizes the media's portrayal of sex and sexual attractiveness, the media often depict adults being carried away by sexual passion, but they do not show that passion leads to coitus, or that coitus leads to pregnancy.

Sex education courses may prevent some, but not many, teenage pregnancies. But it is imperative that teenagers like Susan Carter receive accurate information about their sexuality through such courses for another reason as well. As Susan's comments show, these adolescent girls learned at an early age that they were sexual, but they did not learn about sexuality in a way that would give them a positive sense of being women. . . .

Susan told me about an egg experiment conducted in a former class in lieu of a formal sex education course. As a lesson to deter teen pregnancies, each student was given an egg to care for. They had to give the eggs names and think of them as their newborn babies. The teachers believed that the students would learn about the difficulties of raising children if they had to carry the eggs everywhere and not break them. At the end of the week, the students were to write reports on the responsibility of caring for their "babies." Before the week was over, however, some of the braver students grew tired of the experiment and decided to end it. They took turns rolling their eggs down the corridor yelling, "Crack, baby, crack." The school abandoned the egg experiment after the cracked eggs left a yellow mess on the hallway floor.

Neither the sex education courses nor the egg experiment taught Susan or the other teen girls how to handle the daily sexual advances of the adolescent boys and young men. Access to important information about their sexuality was denied them. Whatever information they could glean was restricted to vague abstractions; the time allocated to its teaching was minimal. Such sex education was ineffective in preventing Susan's pregnancy, let alone addressing the severe social problems that underlie the phenomenon of teenage pregnancy.

A Search for Love and Security

It was late in the evening. Susan and I were comfortable with each other, sitting on the small sofa in the living room, our feet curled up under us. This would be my last visit to Susan's home, and I wanted to ask a few remaining questions.

—*Why do you think you got pregnant?*

Well, it wasn't planned.

—*Did he want you to have a baby before you got pregnant?*

It was unexpected.

—*Did you want to have your baby?*

Yeah.

I usually asked the teen mothers these questions several times, in different ways, throughout the course of our interviews. Often, I realized, they had not decided what they really thought about getting pregnant so young. It was usually during our final discussions that the teen mothers came to grips with their feelings about their pregnancies and about being teenage mothers. When I asked Susan again, she briefly paused before responding: "So . . . um, because it's . . . for a lot of reasons. I didn't want an abortion. I wanted my baby. I just thought . . . I guess I don't really know why (*high-pitched voice*) in some ways." This was the first time she admitted any feelings of confusion.

Susan and I continued our conversation:

—*Perhaps you want something from the baby that you didn't get growing up?*

Susan answered quickly:

Oh, love. She makes me happy. It's fun watching her grow.

—*Did you miss out on something when you were growing up?*

Oh yeah. My mother was too busy working and spending her time elsewhere to care very much about raising me.

Susan's comments tell us that she became pregnant in response to her feeling of alienation from her mother. The only way to handle that feeling was to give birth to a baby, thereby guaranteeing that she receive the love and security she needed. Those comments do not tell the whole story. She did not mention her own uncle's or father's role in this family drama. Nor did she mention how she felt taking classes she did not master. These important details were missing from her final comments, although they helped fill in the story of why fifteen-year-old Susan defied everyone's wish that she have an abortion and sought love and security in motherhood. She did talk about being proud of her relationship with Joney, the baby's father.

Susan talked about Joney in glowing terms, calling him the "most supportive person in my life. He always gave me a lot of support." She informed me that Joney had "class": "He's not a lowlife. It's just that sometimes, his friends, they shoot up and they do crazy stuff." Joney had a history of doing "crazy stuff." She said in a low voice, "I kept telling him, you can't live like that 'cause it's going to catch up to you." It did catch up with him, and he was then serving time in a youth camp. But Susan was sure he would change. She felt confident that when he served his time, he would become the kind of man she wanted him to be. She expected he would find a job as a laborer on his release from the youth camp, because, as Susan put it, "He wants to make it so bad now, and settle down and marry me."

"Did he want the baby?" I wanted to know. Susan responded: "He came to me and said, 'Susan, don't carry my baby if you don't want to. 'Cause if you don't wanna keep it, just give it up for adoption. Whatever you do, that's okay.' He says a lot of things like that. He's so supportive." Susan and I read Joney's comments quite differently. Perhaps because he expressed his views in such negative terms, it struck me that in deciding to have this baby, Susan had taken on all the responsibility for the baby. . . .

A Silent Cry for Help

In some ways Susan's story was about the normal transitional process girls go through during adolescence, when they are learning to handle a changing physiology and the beginning of sexuality identity. In other ways it was about societal pressures, the inadequacy of the sex education being taught to Susan at home and at school, and the freer expression of sexuality she saw in the media and from the boys who were beginning to relate to her in a sexual way. She had no strategies to handle these developmental and social issues.

Having been taught almost nothing about relationships with young men, Susan had no decision-making skill that might help her discern Joney's poor judgments about his lifestyle. At this stage of Susan's life, she was doing what adolescents do: she was basing an attachment on what she saw as Joney's trust and sensitivity. She did not find love and security in her family. Susan's reliance on Joney's support became crucial after her family failed to comprehend the nature of her alienation from school. She began to look for support elsewhere after she was sexually abused for four years by her uncle, after her family failed to take her charges against her uncle seriously, and after she began to have disturbing dreams about that experience.

It was also hard for Susan to navigate the world outside her door. She had no strategy to handle the complexities of growing up in an urban environment ruined by drugs, delinquency, and unemployment.

It is in Susan's description of developmental issues and school and family problems that I have gained a deeper insight into the poverty of these teen mothers' relationships.

COMMON ASSUMPTIONS ABOUT TEEN PREGNANCY AND MOTHERHOOD

Margaret McKinnon, Prue Rains, and Linda Davies

In the following selection, Margaret McKinnon, Prue Rains, and Linda Davies relate common myths and misconceptions about teenage pregnancy and teen mothers. According to the authors, one common misconception is that most teen pregnancies are planned, not accidental. Another frequent assumption, they write, is that teens become pregnant because they have little knowledge about contraception. In fact, the authors maintain, most teens are knowledgeable about contraception but fail to use it consistently. They also point out that some teens become pregnant despite using contraception because the method they chose failed to work. McKinnon is a professor at the University of Ottawa School of Graduate Studies and Research, Rains is a sociology professor at McGill University in Montreal, and Davies is a professor with the McGill University School of Graduate Studies and Research.

Teenage pregnancy is an important issue in several distinct ways. For teenagers themselves, pregnancy often comes as a shock and presents them with a number of difficult decisions, some of which will change their lives, and limited options; so, teenage pregnancy is certainly a significant personal problem. But teenage pregnancy has also been seen in recent years as a significant social problem, worthy of talk-show attention and even government action. The perception is that having large numbers of teen pregnancies is undesirable. It's hard to argue with this view; after all, who wishes to promote teenage pregnancy? Still, teenage pregnancy, while hardly a new phenomenon, did not always attract such attention as a social ill. When abortions were illegal, it was hard to know how many teenagers got them. It was also hard to know how many teenagers got married because they were pregnant; only "unwed mothers" were visible. Teenage pregnancy thus raises important questions about how social issues in general come to our attention and get defined as problems.

What do current statistics indicate about teenage pregnancy? That depends. Interpreting statistics requires making a variety of decisions. Are we interested simply in the *number* of teen pregnancies (which will go up when there are more teenagers) or in *rates* of teen pregnancy? Are we concerned about the issue of *pregnancies* in general, or about teen *births* and teen *mothers* in particular? Are we interested in *married* teenagers or only in *single* ones? And are we looking at all teenagers, up to the age of twenty, or only at those who are younger? And how much younger? Finally, when we examine trends, how long a time-frame shall we look at: broad trends over time, or only recent changes? As you can see, there are difficulties in providing a straightforward set of facts. Nevertheless, here is a very rough overview:

Over the past two decades, more young women have become sexually active and thus at risk of pregnancy. However, in many countries—including Canada—pregnancy rates have not risen, due to great public support for contraceptive use. By contrast, the pregnancy rates for young American women are high. In both countries, despite some variations over time, fewer teenagers are giving birth, due to the legalization and use of abortion. Among those who do give birth, many more are single, a fact that reflects the decline in the use of marriage as a "solution" to pregnancy. Moreover, teenagers who give birth to a child are even more likely now than in the past to keep the child rather than place it for adoption.

Over the past few years, researchers have begun to look more carefully and critically at many of the negative stereotypes and assumptions about teenage pregnancy and teen mothers.

Personal Options

One common myth is that teenagers get pregnant because they don't know about contraception. In reality, teenagers get pregnant for a variety of reasons, just as older women do. Many pregnancies occur in the first six months of sexual activity, or when teenagers discontinue contraceptive use between serious relationships out of concern for the possible health risks of the pill. Most teen pregnancies are accidental, and many happen in spite of contraceptive use, just as they do in older women. Most teenagers are knowledgeable about contraception, although they may not use it consistently. For some teenagers, sex education classes are an important source of information about birth control and the choices to consider when pregnant. However, in many schools contraception and abortion cannot be discussed. As well, access to abortion, birth-control resources and/or pregnancy counselling can vary enormously across Canada and the United States.

Once pregnant, teenagers face limited options, and most worry about how their boyfriends and families will react. Although teenage girls usually turn to their boyfriends and friends, and sometimes parents, for advice, they may keep their situation and their decision private for fear of disapproval. Thus, even though abortion is the most common option chosen (adoption is the least common), the public controversy around abortion has silenced girls from sharing their abortion experiences with one another, leaving each pregnant teenage girl or couple to face the decision on their own. Confronted by the reality of pregnancy, teenagers also find themselves re-evaluating their previous views in the light of their current circumstances. For example, our own research on teen mothers shows very clearly how a girl may reject the idea of an abortion for one pregnancy but accept it for a later one, or the reverse. Although we cannot assume that teenagers will or even should settle ahead of time on which option they *would* choose if they became pregnant, a more open discussion among teenagers about the options is useful.

All Teen Mothers Are Not Victims

Another common assumption about single teen mothers is that their boyfriends have abandoned them. One problem with this image, even when it is an accurate portrayal of the situation, is that it presents the teen mother as the victim of her boyfriend's decisions rather than as an agent with considerations of her own about the relationship. Several studies, including our own, suggest that young women may choose not to marry or live with boyfriends for a variety of reasons. Indeed, the experience of pregnancy itself may lead them to re-examine the relationship and the boyfriend's suitability as a partner and father. And even when teen mothers do not marry, they may live with or continue to be involved with boyfriends who support them in caring for their child, even if not financially.

Another common assumption is that teen mothers are inadequate mothers, either because they have chosen to have a child for the "wrong reasons" and will tire of motherhood, or because they lack the maturity and experience to care properly for a child. Yet some studies show that many teen mothers have had considerable child-care experience and can expect support from their own mothers in caring for their children. Findings like these have sometimes supported a different myth—namely, that teenagers expect their own mothers to assume responsibility for their children. Our research suggests instead that young mothers may regard the responsibility of caring for a child as a path to maturity, even choosing to leave home in order to raise their child more independently. Others, who come from disrupted homes, may experience motherhood as an incentive for "moral reform," leading them to change their lives in order to provide their children with a more stable home life than they had themselves.

Schooling and Welfare

Teen motherhood, and especially single motherhood, is also viewed as a problem because it is assumed that pregnancy and motherhood causes girls to drop out of school, spoiling their future job prospects and hence their ability to support a child without government aid. For some teenagers, dropping out of school in fact precedes their pregnancy and decision to have a child. For them, motherhood and the desire to provide a good future for their child sometimes produces new motivation for returning to school, particularly once their child has reached school age. But, for girls in school, it does indeed seem difficult to combine pregnancy and early motherhood with school work. Some girls are embarrassed to attend school while they are pregnant, and most schools provide little support and make few allowances for mothers. Lack of affordable and reliable day care, transportation costs, and inflexible school schedules and age specifications are among the many difficulties that teen mothers face when they try to go back to school after their child is born.

Under the current circumstances, then, the assumption that teen motherhood will disrupt schooling is not a myth. But it may be worth questioning the assumption that young women should complete their education before starting a family, since this expectation is delaying motherhood for many women well past their twenties, not to mention promoting abortion as a solution to pregnancy among college-going women. Social policies that support young women's desire for both an education *and* a family, and a greater range of choices for combining the two, are thus worth considering. An example of such a progressive policy is provided by schools that have developed special programs, including on-site day care, to help teen mothers return to and stay in school.

Finally, another common assumption is that teen mothers have chosen to have babies in order to get access to welfare benefits. As we have said before, most pregnancies are not deliberately planned, but accidental. Studies suggest that welfare may nonetheless be an important source of income for young mothers. While they might see welfare as a temporary option, however, few plan to spend their lives on it. Like older mothers, they find that it is hard to live on meagre welfare allowances, even to cover basic necessities. But given the unreliability of low-paid jobs, along with the additional costs of child care, the teen mothers we interviewed often concluded that staying on welfare was the more responsible course of action while their child was of pre-school age.

A Serious Social Problem: Teen Girls and Older Men

Oliver Starr Jr.

Oliver Starr Jr. focuses on the social and economic implications of the exploitation of teenage girls by adult men. According to a study conducted by the California Department of Health in the early 1990s, he writes, men over twenty years of age fathered more than three-quarters of the babies born to teen mothers. Starr also points to evidence that many men coerce or intimidate their younger girlfriends into having abortions. Those young women who do have their babies often receive no financial or emotional support from their child's father, he reveals. Starr is a freelance writer and former editor for the *St. Louis Globe-Democrat*.

The exploitation of teenage girls by older men may be one of the nation's most serious social problems, but it seldom is written or talked about. Approximately 900,000 teenage girls become pregnant each year; a little more than half of them give birth. The conventional wisdom is that their classmates father nearly all of these children. But a 1992 California Department of Health Services study showed that more than three-quarters of these children were fathered by men older than 20 and more than 70 percent of the births were out of wedlock. The study further found that men older than 20 also father five times more births among junior-high-school girls than do junior-high-school boys.

For girls in junior high, the father is on average 6.5 years older. When the mother is 12 years old or younger, the father averages 22. Most of these older fathers abandon their "used girls" like so many vessels of spoiled meat after getting them pregnant.

"These studies highlight the problem that a substantial portion of teenage sexual activity is more a matter of manipulation, coercion or abuse than anything else," wrote Joe S. McIlhaney, gynecologist and expert on sexually transmitted diseases, in *Insight on the News* (September 29, 1997).

The 1996 "Kids Having Kids" study by the Robin Hood Foundation, a community-based relief agency in New York City, reached a similar conclusion. It says its research, conducted by leading scholars, "suggests that the incidence of pregnancy among adolescent girls often is a result of sexually predatory behavior of older men."

"Research also shows that about 25 percent of girls who become pregnant get that way under the influence of drugs and alcohol," says McIlhaney, founder of the Medical Institute of Sexual Health in Austin, Texas. "And we know how intense peer pressure is. It's a pit, a cesspool. Teens are not having 'beautiful, consensual sex' as is portrayed in films and TV. They are having horrible, manipulative sex that is saturated with drugs, alcohol and loneliness."

A Pattern of Coercion in Abortions

Studies of the causes of abortions show a continuing pattern of abuse. Steve Schwalm, former senior writer and analyst at the Family Research Council in Washington, recounts in the Knight-Ridder/Tribune News the case of a young pregnant woman and her boyfriend that occurred in August 1997 at the Hillcrest Women's Surgi-Center in Washington—not too far from the White House—where she planned to have an abortion.

Responding to the plea of a man outside the clinic "to love her baby and not go in," she abruptly changed her mind and sat down on a red brick wall as her boyfriend continued inside. In seconds, he returned and badgered her for about a half-hour, trying to make her go in for the abortion. She refused.

The boyfriend "then hit the woman on the face and she tumbled to the ground. He continued beating her in the face and then sat on her and beat her some more, according to police, until clinic workers lifted her up and took her into the abortion center," Schwalm reported.

One would have expected an outcry not just in Washington but nationally about this pregnant woman being so savagely beaten by the baby's father, trying to force her to have an abortion. But there was no outcry, "not even a mention of this incident by groups ostensibly founded to defend women's rights," says Schwalm.

It turns out that this kind of abusive behavior by boyfriends toward women and girls they have impregnated is common and goes largely unreported by the media. The following data cited by Schwalm shows a pattern of coercion in abortions, refuting the common view that they almost always are consensual:

- The Elliot Institute reports that about 40 percent of abortion cases involve coercion.
- A survey of members of the organization Women Exploited by Abortion showed 33 percent were encouraged to have abortions by their boyfriends—higher than even the percentage (27 percent) pushed in that direction by abortion counselors.
- Fifty-four percent of the respondents also said they felt "forced by outside circumstances" to have an abortion.
- Husbands pushed for abortion the least, at only 9 percent.

A High Incidence of Sexually Transmitted Disease

The media also seldom mention the venereal-disease epidemic plaguing the nation and hitting teenagers particularly hard. Three million teenage girls and boys—approximately 20 percent of teens who are sexually active—become infected with a sexually transmitted disease every year.

How disproportionate this is to the adult population can be seen in the fact that teenagers account for 25 percent of all cases of sexually transmitted diseases even though they make up only about 10 percent of the population. AIDS commonly is thought to seldom strike the young, but the National Institutes of Allergy and Infectious Disease in 1996 found that 25 percent of all new HIV infections in the United States are estimated to occur in young people between ages 13 and 20.

So little has been reported about the VD epidemic that the Institute of Medicine titled its 1997 report on the outbreak *The Hidden Epidemic—Confronting Sexually Transmitted Disease.* Federal and local public-health officials say "the United States is in the throes of an epidemic of sexually transmitted diseases that in poor, underserved areas such as Baltimore's inner city rivals that of some developing nations," Sheryl Gay Stolberg reported in the *New York Times* in March 1999.

King K. Holmes, professor of medicine at the University of Washington, says that a "conspiracy of silence" has allowed sexually transmitted infections to flourish. The number of new sexual-disease cases each year has increased from 10 million to 12 million. These include high rates of human papilloma virus, chlamydia and herpes—as well as serious local outbreaks of syphilis and gonorrhea.

"A study released last October [1997] found that one in five Americans older than 12 was infected with the genital herpes virus, a 30 percent increase from two decades ago. Rates among white teenagers quadrupled," she said.

The evidence points once more to men older than 20 as major spreaders of venereal disease among teenage girls. The Centers for Disease Control and Prevention in 1996 warned: "These adult/youth sex patterns have profound implications for the spread of sexually transmitted disease, or STD, and AIDS as well. STD and AIDS rates are 2.5 times higher among females under age 20 than can be predicted from rates among males under age 20. . . . This points strongly to STD transmission from older men."

Social and Economic Costs Are High

Most of the older-than-20 men and high-school boys who father these out-of-wedlock children also refuse to provide any kind of support, financial or otherwise, for the teenage girls they impregnate or their children. "More than half of teenage mothers are not residing with their child's father by the time the child reaches grade school. More than one-quarter have never lived with the father," Suzanne

Chazin reported in *Reader's Digest.* "Nor does the father offer much (financial) help: only 20 percent of never-married mothers receive formal child support, according to the Congressional Budget Office."

The social and economic costs of these teenage-pregnancy, abortion and STD epidemics are enormous. They have been estimated to run as high as $21 billion a year. Taking care of a baby without the help of the father is a full-time job, often preventing the teenage mother from earning money she needs to support herself and the child, which is why eight out of 10 of these girls go on welfare, where a great many of them and their children often remain for a generation or more.

Dependent families formed by teenage mothers consume more than half of all welfare money spent. Nearly 30 percent of unmarried mothers stay poor during their twenties and thirties, the critically important developmental years of their children. Only three of 10 girls who become pregnant at the age of 17 or younger will earn a high-school diploma by age 30, as contrasted with 76 percent of women who delay childbearing until the age of 20 or older, according to the "Kids Having Kids" study.

Children of unmarried teenage girls also have much more severe problems than children of married parents. The same study points out:

- Teenage sons of adolescent mothers are 2.7 times more likely to go to prison than the sons of mothers who delay childbearing until their early twenties.
- Children of teenage mothers have more trouble in school. They perform significantly worse on tests.
- Performance in school does not improve as children of adolescent mothers age; they are far more likely to drop out than are children born to later childbearers.

Teenage Girls Need to Learn

It is ironic that a society that vigorously prosecutes hit-and-run drivers does so little to stop the impregnate-and-run men who cumulatively have ruined the lives of many millions of teenage girls by making them pregnant and then taking off for parts unknown.

Despite their unsavory, predatory record, the disappearing deadbeat dads of out-of-wedlock children seem to find another bumper crop of teenage girls each year willing to rush into their arms for a trip down nightmare alley and poverty row. . . . Somehow, teenage girls have got to get the message that going out with these older men is like the proverbial fly's acceptance to visit the spider's web.

PREGNANT BY DESIGN

Allison Bell

In the following selection, Allison Bell provides insights on teens who choose to become pregnant. According to Bell, about 15 percent of teens who get pregnant each year do so on purpose. Their reasons for wanting to be pregnant vary, she writes, from the means of keeping a boyfriend to the need for attention to the desire for a baby to give their life love and meaning. In Bell's view, getting pregnant without being married has become much more acceptable in recent years. She notes that some school and government programs intended to help pregnant teens may inadvertently provide teens with incentives for getting pregnant. However, Bell cautions, even teens who become pregnant on purpose often find that being a teen mother is more difficult than anticipated and wish they had waited until they were older. Bell is a contributing editor for *Teen* magazine.

We hear a lot about girls who accidentally become pregnant, but you might be surprised to learn some teen moms actually plan their pregnancies. Considering how tough it is to be a teen mother, it's hard to imagine that any girl would choose to be one, but some do. Why? What motivates them? Would they do it again after discovering what life with a baby is like?

Getting Pregnant on Purpose

Sandra Lucero was just 13—some would say a baby herself—when she first fantasized about having a child. She got kind of obsessed with the idea, and even started faking it. "I'd tell people, 'I'm pregnant; and they'd get all excited and say, 'Gosh, how many months are you?'" the 19-year-old from Anaheim Hills, California, recalls. She'd bask in the attention—until it was evident her tummy wasn't getting any bigger. Then she'd tell everyone the pregnancy test was wrong.

Three years later, however, Sandra did become pregnant—for real— through unprotected sex with her boyfriend, who was four years older. While getting pregnant wasn't something she'd actually sat down and discussed with him, in the back of her mind Sandra hoped

Reprinted from Allison Bell, "Pregnant on Purpose," *Teen*, August 1997. Reprinted with permission from *Teen*.

it would happen. "I was feeling so insecure about everything, I thought being pregnant and having a cute little baby to hold would make me feel better," she says.

After dropping out of school, Sandra thought she'd spend her time blissing out, awaiting the child she hoped would give her life meaning. But in reality she moved into a cramped apartment with her boyfriend—and his mom—where she mostly did a whole lot of nothing. Soon, Sandra started to feel fat, ugly and, despite the close quarters, terribly alone and unloved. "It wasn't the way it was supposed to be," she says.

A lot of teens get pregnant by mistake, and they make up the majority of teen moms. Out of the almost 1 million teenage girls who become pregnant each year, 85 percent don't plan their pregnancy, according to the Alan Guttmacher Institute, a nonprofit reproductive health corporation in New York that tracks teen pregnancy trends. As for the other 15 percent, those pregnancies are intentional.

Maybe girls who get pregnant on purpose don't do their research. For one thing, teen moms often receive poor prenatal care and they face higher complications. Babies born to young mothers are prone to low birth weight and other health problems. Plus, about a third of teen moms live in poverty—and even if they finish high school, they're less likely to go to college or get a good job.

Yet even if they have a clue that motherhood can be tough, some girls go for it anyway; perhaps their romantic ideas outweigh the real-life rigors. "There are girls motivated by the idea that having a baby will give them the love or sense of hope they feel is missing," says Donna Butts, executive director of the National Organization on Adolescent Pregnancy, Parenting and Prevention (NOAPPP) in Washington, D.C. "And some view having a baby as an insurance policy on keeping their boyfriends."

Although that tactic rarely works—ironically, Butts says, most of the fathers check out shortly after the baby arrives—Sandra bought into the idea.

Incentives for Pregnancy

Teen pregnancy cuts across all cultures and economic lines. Seventy-six percent of teen pregnancies occur outside wedlock, but the other 24 percent of teen moms are married. Often, these girls see marriage and babies as their only option in life. Many teens become pregnant to feel validated, says Regina Law, young parents program coordinator for Friends of the Family, a non-profit counseling agency in Van Nuys, California. "I see girls 14 or 16 who are either married or living with their boyfriends—they see getting pregnant as the next logical step."

May—who asked that her last name not be used—is one example. She was 16, the daughter of strict Chinese parents, when she fell for a 26-year-old Vietnamese guy. Her parents disapproved not of his age but of his nationality; they wanted May to marry Chinese. So, partly to get her parents to accept him, May and her boyfriend of only five months decided to have a baby.

Their plan worked. Once she was pregnant, May's parents agreed to let her marry her boyfriend (in most states, minors need parental permission to marry). May quit school and moved in with her new husband.

Could it be that girls who want babies feel freer to do so today than in the past? In general, it seems that being an "unwed mother" is less of a taboo in society's eyes than it used to be.

At some schools, it's considered cool to be 16 with a bulging belly. Take the small, middle-class town of Tipton, Indiana. "Teen pregnancy is not looked poorly upon by peers here," says William Stone, M.D., an obstetrician who cofounded Teen Pregnancy Coalition to help stem the rising teen pregnancy rate in his town. "In fact, it's greeted with a great deal of excitement."

Schools have become much more teen-mother friendly, too. Some offer on-campus day care centers, lifesavers for teen moms who might otherwise have to drop out of school to care for their children. Some people argue, however, that these high-school day care centers are sending the wrong message to teens—that they encourage young girls to get pregnant. "There is this mixed message that the community is sending," Stone says.

Schools aren't the only institutions providing aid for young moms: If a girl is on welfare, the government also lends a hand. "There are many programs that take good care of teen mothers—but the down side is, it makes getting pregnant almost look attractive," says Priscilla Hurley, executive director of Teen Awareness Inc./Choices, a Fullerton, California–based sexuality instruction program that emphasizes personal responsibility and abstinence. One attractive parenting program in Hurley's area is Cal-Learn. As long as the girl is getting high school credit, the program pays for day care, mileage for school and job-training travel, books and uniforms. Pama Tavernier, an Orange County social worker with the program, has seen Cal-Learn turn girls' lives around, but even she wonders if the perks may give girls "an incentive to get pregnant."

Surprisingly, the incentive also comes from parents. "Usually the girl's mother is young herself, so she's happy to accept a baby in her life, allowing her daughter to continue her social and school activities," Stone says.

Reality Bites

While girls may plan pregnancies with high hopes, reality seldom matches the fantasy. In fact, Sandra felt so isolated that she followed her boyfriend everywhere—even into the bathroom. In her ninth month, "he asked me to leave," Sandra says. She went home to her parents and had her son. At first, Sandra spent her days flipping burgers at a local restaurant, and her nights changing diapers and washing bottles. Now she lives in an apartment with a roommate and barely gets by on the meager payments from Aid to Families with Dependent Children (AFDC). Although she's gone back to school, Sandra wonders if she and her 2-year-old son will survive until she's able to bring home a bigger paycheck.

It's been just slightly easier for May, who now has two sons. She and her husband are still together and they're both attending school and looking forward to the day when they won't have to rely on federal assistance. "It's been a rough time," she says. "If I had to do it over again, I'd take it a lot more slowly."

While the number of babies born to teens has declined slightly in recent years, the teen pregnancy rate is still alarmingly high, and teenage moms face tough obstacles:

Teen pregnancy rates are much higher in the United States than in many other developed countries. The rate is twice as high as in England, Wales and Canada, and nine times as high as in the Netherlands and Japan.

Each year, 11 percent of all girls ages 15 to 19 become pregnant. About four in 10 teen girls will get pregnant before they turn 20.

About 8 percent of 14-year-old girls, 18 percent of 15- to 17-year-olds and 22 percent of 18- to 19-year-olds become pregnant each year.

Twenty-eight percent of teen mothers now in their 20s and early 30s live at the poverty level; only 7 percent of women who first give birth after adolescence are poor at these ages.

DO TEEN FATHERS DESERVE THEIR BAD IMAGE?

Larry Muhammad

According to Larry Muhammad, the commonly held image of teenage fathers as uncaring and irresponsible is false. To support his contention, he cites the findings of a number of experts that most teenage fathers provide some financial support and have daily contact with their children even if they do not live with them. He also looks at two teenage fathers who chose to honor their commitment as parents even though this decision has meant sacrifices and lifestyle changes on their part. Muhammad writes that much of the bad image associated with teen fathers actually belongs to adult men, who are responsible for the majority of teen pregnancies. Pointing out that research shows that fathers are key to successful childrearing, he describes various initiatives available to assist teenage fathers. Muhammad is a staff writer for the *Courier-Journal* in Louisville, Kentucky.

When Kontar Roberson was a junior at Moore Traditional High School in Louisville, Kentucky, he got some news that changed his life: His girlfriend, Marja Ellis, a sophomore at Central High in Louisville, was pregnant with his child.

"He quit school, got a job, rented us an apartment at $535 a month, helped with my expenses and bought everything the baby needed," Ellis said.

Exposing a False Image

Now 19 and a pizza cook, Roberson said teachers and parents advised him to finish school, but "I didn't listen. I was young and dumb. I wanted to take care of my responsibilities. Now I get up in the morning and the first thing I see is my daughter, hitting me in the face, or putting her bottle up my nose. It's fun doing stuff with her. Everything I wanted to do when I was young and didn't do, I get to do with her."

On cool summer evenings, Roberson and Ellis, an 18-year-old bank teller and Central graduate, look the perfect couple, pushing

Reprinted from Larry Muhammad, "Teen Dads: Image of Them as Irresponsible or Invisible Is Wrong," *The Louisville Courier-Journal*, June 20, 1999. Reprinted with permission from *The Louisville Courier-Journal*.

their year-old daughter, Sasathia, through their neighborhood in her carriage.

But there are no illusions.

"This wasn't planned," said Ellis, "and if I had it to do all over again, I wouldn't get pregnant. Your whole childhood is taken away."

Abortion was out of the question.

"We weren't killing no babies," Roberson said. "And none of my buddies told me to run off. They said, 'Aw, man, you got a baby? You know you gotta do the right thing.' Even if they hadn't, I figured, 'I love this girl, she's having my baby, and I'm going to be there.'"

If Roberson confounds the popular image of the sexually precocious teen-ager too irresponsible and self-absorbed to care about the child he fathers, that's because the image is false.

Psychologists and family therapists say that Roberson actually is typical and that the parental commitment and sacrifices of fathers his age are routinely overlooked in efforts to track down "deadbeat" dads.

"The stereotype of the young teen father who had made pregnant 14 girls is really just wrong," said Maureen Pirog, professor of public policy at Indiana University. She completed a four-year study of 1,000 teen-age fathers in 1995. "Most of these boys had sex with their girl-friend. They didn't have children with four or five different women, and when that occurred, it was really a rarity. And they left high school to go to work soon after the child was born or right before."

The first nationwide study of underage fathers, sponsored by the Ford Foundation in 1985, found that 82 percent had daily contact with their children despite living apart, 74 percent helped financially support their children and 90 percent kept contact with the mothers.

Says Mark Kiselica, an adolescent psychologist in Newtown, Pennsylvania, and author of *Multicultural Counseling with Teenage Fathers:* "Seventy percent of the guys who are responsible for teen pregnancies are adult men; they're in their 20s. So a lot of the images we have about teen fathers are confused with the older guys. And if you examine the studies that have carefully focused on the boys involved, in their teen-age years, you can roughly speaking say that most of the guys have a long-term relationship with the girl."

Teen Parenthood Is Tough

Teen-age pregnancy has colossal social and financial costs, absorbing millions of dollars yearly in Louisville-area services and billions every year nationwide.

Most teen-age mothers don't finish high school or marry. They are less likely to get prenatal care, so more of their babies are born prematurely and underweight.

Even an ideal pregnancy and a healthy child to raise usually are more than adolescents can handle.

Says Ellis, "I see 14-year-old mothers with their babies in the doctor's office. She can't even take her own kid to the doctor's. Her mom's got to do it, because she's a kid herself."

Nineteen-year-old homemaker Christina Turner dropped out of Shawnee High in Louisville when she got pregnant with her son, Anthony Turner, now 2. Times were tough even though she had the love and support of her baby's father, 18-year-old Wayne Simpson, who dropped out of Western High in Louisville and did restaurant maintenance work to pay the bills.

"We moved in with my mom until Anthony turned 5 months," Turner says. "I was drawing welfare at the time, and they tried to push him for child support, but when I moved out they cut me right off. Now that we're on our own, we've got to go to court and show rent receipts and all that to prove he's taking care of his responsibility."

Turner is five months pregnant with their second child. She doesn't work and the family lives on Simpson's salary, sharing a one-bedroom apartment where their friends—Simpson's buddies and other young mothers who know Turner—often stop by.

They have a pit-bull puppy, Tipsy, which their son played with in their yard one evening in June 1999, splashing in a portable wading pool Simpson was filling with a garden hose.

"We're looking for a nicer apartment," said Simpson, but the chances of his being able to afford it seem slim.

Carefree Days Are Gone

Says Pirog, "Teen fathers make whatever they can early on—and more than kids in school. But kids who stay in school and go to college end up earning a lot more, and the earning gap gets bigger and bigger."

Roberson says he's going back to school once his daughter is old enough for day care, and Ellis says she plans to pursue a nursing career.

Right now they live in a two-bedroom apartment, but like most parents with a young child, both work to make ends meet and their free time is devoted to Sasathia. They share household chores and work alternate shifts—Roberson nights and Ellis days—so one of them is always home with the baby.

The couple prize their financial independence and say they've always had the moral support of their parents, though sometimes they do miss just being carefree kids.

"I miss hanging out late, going to the park and playing ball with my friends," Roberson says.

"I miss amusement parks, chilling with my friends," Ellis says.

Focusing on Teen-Age Fathers

The number of teen-age pregnancies appears to have leveled off and slightly declined.

According to statistics from the Kentucky Department of Public

Health, babies born to girls 15 to 19 numbered 9,438, or about 17.5 percent of the total 54,041 births statewide in 1990, and 8,620, or about 16 percent of a total 52,843 births, in 1997, the last year for which figures are available.

In about 20 percent of Kentucky births, the father wasn't identified. But babies born to boys 15 to 19 were about 3 percent of the total for both years: 1,691 in 1990, 1,672 in 1997.

These are the youngsters experts say are more prone to squarely face the consequences of fathering a child out of wedlock. That's important; research shows that fathers are key to successful child rearing and that antisocial behavior in youngsters is sometimes linked to female-headed, single-parent homes.

Prevention of teen-age pregnancy remains a hallmark of public policy. The Child Support Division of the Kentucky Cabinet for Families and Children, for example, is aiming an abstinence campaign at boys. It includes "It's Official," a 19-minute video dramatizing the difficulties and consequences of having a child from the teen perspective, and a series of six "male responsibility" posters. One shows a chicken and a caption reading, "What do you call a guy who makes a baby and then flies the coop?" In another, a young father prepares his son for a baby carriage, and the caption reads, "This isn't the convertible you were saving for."

Where prevention fails, help is available to teen-age fathers. Books such as *Teen Dads* by Jeanne Warren Lindsay instruct underage fathers on everything from assisting in labor and delivery to nurturing a newborn and charting a family future.

Says Kathy Adams, spokesman for Kentucky's state child support division, "Child support historically has a reputation for chasing down deadbeat dads. We've tried of late to change that approach a little. We need to support fathers who stay involved with their kids."

For six years, until 1993, the Teenage Parent Program of the Jefferson County Public Schools in Kentucky helped 150 adolescent fathers each year with financial planning and parenting skills in a pilot program called the Fatherhood Project.

"We lost the funding," said coordinator Sara York, "so we don't have a full-time person to recruit the fathers into the program so we can help them. But also we were finding more and more older fathers. The focus of the group was on teen fathers, and the fathers were 23 and 24."

Pirog called for more initiatives for teen-age fathers. "Intervention programs really ought to try and get in there very early, before the baby is born, to help them cope," Pirog said. "These are big decisions, major life events that even an adult would have a problem with."

Roberson says he doesn't mind the sacrifice and is proud to be a father.

"OK, yeah, we sneaked around and had sex," he said. "But I'm taking care of my kid. She ain't sick. She gets whatever she wants, and ain't never been on welfare."

Says Simpson of raising his son, Anthony, "It's easier now. He's out of diapers and through with formula. But my dad . . . left when I wasn't even a year old, and I haven't seen him since. I wanted to show him I was a man, and he wasn't."

CHAPTER 2

PREVENTING AND REDUCING TEEN PREGNANCY

Contemporary Issues
Companion

THE ULTIMATE GOAL: PREVENTING TEEN PREGNANCY

Paula Edelson

Paula Edelson is the author of *Straight Talk About Teenage Pregnancy*, from which the following article is taken. Edelson describes a number of initiatives and programs designed to prevent teen pregnancy. For example, she writes that the U.S. Department of Health and Human Services is promoting a national strategy that utilizes such tactics as community-based prevention programs that advocate parental involvement and abstinence. Edelson also describes such federally funded initiatives as the Adolescent Family Life program, an organization that supports projects advocating abstinence. According to Edelson, abstinence is the only sure way to prevent pregnancy.

Tess's baby was adopted by a family in another state. She thinks about her little boy all the time and feels sad when she realizes that she won't be there to watch him grow up—to see who he looks like, what makes him laugh, and what he likes to do for fun. At the same time, Tess is happy that her son is with a loving family—one that can do much more for him than she can.

What really disturbs Tess is seeing all the teenage girls in her neighborhood who are pregnant now. They act so overconfident, even cocky. Then there are the girls who are just beginning to go out with guys. Tess doesn't know them well enough to say anything to them, but if she did, she'd tell them to be careful. Pregnancy *is* a big deal. It changes your life, and makes it much harder. . . .

The good news about teen pregnancy is that it's on the decline. According to a 1997 study by the National Center for Health Statistics, teenage birthrates nationwide have diminished substantially from 1991 to 1996. The reason for this trend is unclear. Some credit a focus in education on the need to remain abstinent before marriage. "We believe abstinence has played the central role in what's happening," Amy Stephens, a spokeswoman for the pro-abstinence organization Focus in the Family, told the *New York Times* in a May 1, 1998 article. "Kids respond when they get a direct message [to remain absti-

Excerpted from Paula Edelson, *Straight Talk About Teenage Pregnancy*. Copyright ©1998 Paula Edelson. Reprinted with permission from Facts On File, Inc.

nent] instead of the mixed message that if you're going to have sex, you should use a condom, but oh, also, we don't think you should have sex." On the other hand, other groups stress that the proper use of contraceptives has been the key to the diminishing rate of teen pregnancy in the United States. "We're seeing the result of more widespread and more effective contraceptive use," Jacqueline E. Darroch, senior vice president for research at the Alan Guttmacher Institute, told the *New York Times* in the same article.

Even so, both national and community leaders believe that more work has to be done to bring down the rate of teen pregnancy even further. The keys to success, many strategists believe, is to offer a positive message to teenagers—one that stresses the advantages of postponing not only parenthood, but sexual involvement as well. . . .

The National Strategy to Prevent Teen Pregnancy

In 1995 President Bill Clinton announced that the issue of teen pregnancy was a crucial one sorely in need of attention. He voiced concern not only for the social cost of teen pregnancy but for its effects on both adolescent parents and their children. Clinton put his vision in specific terms: He strives to cut teen pregnancy rates by 33 percent by the year 2006.

With this mission in mind, the U.S. Department of Health and Human Services has issued a national strategy to achieve two specific goals. First, it stresses the need to encourage teenagers to avoid teen pregnancy. Second, it strives to use both local and national initiatives to remind teenagers that staying in school, delaying sexual intercourse, and preparing for work are, in the long run, the best things to do.

The U.S. Department of Health's strategy stresses that the best way to prevent teen pregnancy is to carry out the following five principles through community-based prevention programs.

1) Parental and adult involvement: Increased communication between teenagers and trusted adults is key.
2) Abstinence: Any prevention program, the strategy stresses, must begin with a strong message to delay sexual intercourse.
3) Clear strategies for the future: Young people must be given realistic and attainable opportunities to attend college and pursue jobs.
4) Community involvement: The strategy stresses that all facets of a community—including parents, schools, businesses, media, health and human services providers, religious organizations, and of course, teenagers themselves—must work together to develop realistic and comprehensive prevention approaches.
5) Sustained commitment: Nothing works overnight. True success will come only if these principles are followed over a period of time.

The welfare law signed by President Clinton in 1996 includes specific policies for adolescent parents. In particular, it states that all teen mothers must live at home and stay in school in order to receive governmental assistance. The law also provides for Second Chance Homes, a program for teenagers at risk of being abused if they stay with their parents. The idea behind this program is to provide supervised group residences for teen mothers from abusive or unstable homes to live with their children. With money and guidance from the federal government, the homes provide socialization, nurturing, support, structure, and discipline for these young mothers and their children. All mothers who live in the Second Chance Homes network do qualify for welfare assistance.

In addition, the welfare law provides $50 million a year to fund state abstinence-education programs. This means that there will be more tools available to help teenagers make informed, responsible decisions to delay sexual intercourse until they are older.

Finally, the new policy intends to send a strong message to teenagers that parenthood does involve responsibility and obligations. With this goal in mind, the law includes measures to name the father in every case of teen pregnancy and to prosecute those fathers who are not paying proper child support. . . .

Government, State, and Community Initiatives

For a project at school, Tess is trying to learn all she can about what the U.S. government is doing to try to limit the number of teen pregnancies in the United States. . . .

Tess has found that there are a number of initiatives that are funded by the federal government, and the good news is that teenagers don't have to go to Washington, D.C. in order to benefit from the programs because there are branches of these programs in communities all over the United States. The initiatives focus not only on preventing pregnancy but on helping teenagers who are already pregnant or have children by providing them information and services.

For example, the Adolescent Family Life program is an organization that supports projects to advocate abstinence. The AFL puts this first on its agenda because abstinence is the only sure way to prevent not only pregnancy but the spread of all sexually transmitted diseases. But as Tess knows, many teenagers do have sexual intercourse. What about services for them? Tess was happy to find that the AFL also offers some health, education, and social services to teen mothers who are either pregnant or already parents, as well as to their infants, male partners, and families. (It's important to note, however, that current restrictions do not allow any federally funded family planning services to discuss the option of abortion.) Finally, the AFL sponsors in 14 states projects that are specifically designed to reduce repeat teen pregnancy through education. . . .

The government is taking steps to implement programs in schools as well as in community centers. One initiative, called Healthy

Schools, Healthy Communities, has established health centers in schools in 27 communities in 20 states and the District of Columbia. These centers provide a wide range of educational and health-related services for teenagers who are considered at a high risk of becoming pregnant. There are also community school programs, again funded by the federal government, that support activities during nonschool hours for young people in communities that have a high number of pregnant teenagers. Finally, there are funded school programs designed specifically to reduce early sexual activity and abuse of tobacco, alcohol, and illicit drugs.

Tess has also found other government initiatives, such as those that help teenagers deal with substance abuse, and some hot lines for pregnant teens that she knows will be helpful for teenagers. But she also feels that any successful effort to reduce teen pregnancy really needs to begin on the community, or grassroots, level. That way, community residents are involved from the beginning. . . .

It's true that the most important strategies for pregnancy prevention are not the ones that originate in Washington, D.C., but the ones that happen at the grassroots level. The idea behind grassroots projects is to help provide opportunities for the community's teenagers to be educated about pregnancy and also to provide options for them and their future. In other words, successful community programs to reduce teenage pregnancy aim to provide teenagers with hope and opportunity. One reason teenagers get pregnant may be out of a sense of hopelessness. Perhaps if teenagers are provided with some guidance and support, fewer teenagers will resort to pregnancy as a "quick fix" to relieve the pain and hopelessness about their future that they may be feeling.

With these goals in mind, several communities have started innovative programs to help their teenage residents. For example, the Washington State Department of Health has spearheaded the Teen Pregnancy Prevention Media Campaign. This program, according to the website of Washington's Ferndale High School, had five specific goals:

- "To develop a sense of responsibility, commitment, and ownership of the issue in individual communities across the state.
- To encourage teens to delay sexual activity or to use contraceptives if they are already sexually active.
- To provide information to the public regarding the facts and issues about teen pregnancy.
- To encourage parents and other influential adults to exercise responsibility for their children's behavior.
- To promote collaboration and communication among schools, community organizations, and private partnerships, including cross training, joint planning, and resource pooling."

In order to meet these ambitions, the campaign will use several different media outlets: radio commercials developed by teens and conveying specific messages, such as the consequences of early sexual activity, to be played on popular teen stations; tabloid inserts and advertisements on teen issues, to be published in a popular teen newspaper; and televised town hall meetings on teen issues, including parent-teen communication and responsible sexual behavior.

There are some other innovative community programs as well. For example, in New York City Dr. Michael Carrera has initiated a pregnancy prevention program that provides tutoring, college tuition, and classes in sex and health education to participating teenagers. His program, which has been adopted in several other states, is based on the positive philosophy that the way to help teenagers avoid pregnancy is to offer them opportunities that give them hope and possibilities for a better future.

Another promising campaign to reduce pregnancy is under way in Arkansas, where the media have spearheaded a statewide effort to alert residents about the problem of teen pregnancy and to encourage them to take preventative action. With this goal in mind, the state has implemented prevention and parenting programs in five communities. One program focuses on ways parents can talk to their children about sex. Another offers pregnancy prevention workshops to male teenagers and young adults. A third strives to prevent second pregnancies through employment opportunities and self-esteem classes.

New Legislative Measures

Many lawmakers believe that the best way to prevent teen pregnancy is to make it harder for teen parents to receive the benefits they have always counted on to help them raise their children, such as welfare, for example. In addition, these lawmakers believe that punishing teens and young adults for their actions will serve as a useful prevention technique. Several states have taken action to test this theory. For example,

- In Iowa, all teen parents are required by law to live at home or under adult supervision. In addition, they must attend parenting classes, complete high school, and participate in PROMISE JOBS, Iowa's job training program.
- In Maryland, legislation is pending that would require all unmarried teen parents to live under adult supervision.
- California has established the Underage Sex Offense Unit, which investigates and prosecutes adult males who impregnate teenagers and younger girls.
- In Florida, legislation is pending that would charge a man over 18 who has impregnated a girl under the age of 15 with second-degree statutory rape. The offender would be responsible for child support and medical costs related to pregnancy. . . .

Teens Hold the Solution

Keep in mind that it is very difficult to change the realities of life in the inner cities and in rural towns with few activities—to offer teenagers and others a way out of what they may find to be a depressing and unbearable way of life.

At the same time, don't lose sight of the fact that it can be done. Options do exist for impoverished teenagers, mainly in the form of education and community activities. . . .

It's important to remember that the real prevention strategy for teen pregnancy is not found in either communities or federal programs. Instead, it is ultimately within the control of teenagers themselves to decide what they want to do and how they want to live their lives.

Moving to Curb Teen Pregnancy

School Board News

In the following selection, the editors of *School Board News* report on a 1998 forum concerning teen pregnancy, which was sponsored by the National School Boards Association and the National Association of State Boards of Education. According to presenters at the forum, the United States has the highest rate of teen pregnancies of any industrialized nation in the world. In their view, reducing this rate requires a comprehensive approach that includes such elements as early intervention, sexuality education, counseling, and health services. Forum participants advocate long-term programs, suggesting that educators adopt prevention programs that have been successful in other schools. These experts also agree that it is essential to challenge the prevalent belief among young people that teen pregnancy is acceptable.

"Most teens are not ready financially or emotionally to have a child. Teens don't realize that," says Ventura Washington, a student at Wakefield High School in Arlington, Virginia.

"Teens are careless and do not realize the consequences of sexual activity. It's hard to be a teen parent. Many teens do not realize that," says Sothea Kim, who attends an alternative high school program in Arlington while her own parents care for her 18-month-old daughter.

A Comprehensive Strategy Is Needed

The difficulty of convincing teenagers to understand the consequence of their behavior is one of the top challenges facing school leaders concerned with reducing teenage pregnancy rates.

Both teens quoted above were part of a panel of teens who spoke candidly about their lives at a forum on preventing teen pregnancy in Washington, D.C., December 9–10, 1998.

The forum, sponsored by the National School Boards Association (NSBA) and the National Association of State Boards of Education (NASBE), was funded by the Centers for Disease Control and Prevention (CDC).

Forum participants—members of state and local boards of educa-

Reprinted from *School Board News*, "Preventing Teen Pregnancy Requires Comprehensive Approach," December 22, 1998. Reprinted with permission from the National School Boards Association.

tion—identified policy actions to accomplish the twin goals of improving student achievement and reducing teen pregnancy.

There was general consensus among the forum presenters that reducing the teen pregnancy rate requires a comprehensive strategy that includes several elements—early intervention, sexuality education, counseling, health services, and youth development. And many spoke about the need for collaborative efforts among various organizations.

Echoing the sentiments of many conference participants, Cathy Melvin, chief of the program services and development branch in the CDC's Division of Reproduction Health, said: "The current evidence indicates that reducing adolescent pregnancy is possible but challenging."

While the teen pregnancy rate is going down, the United States still has the highest rate of any industrialized nation. Nearly one million girls get pregnant each year in the United States, reports the National Campaign to Prevent Teen Pregnancy.

Or, to put it another way, "every 26 seconds, another adolescent gets pregnant," says Gerald Tirozzi, assistant secretary for elementary and secondary education at the U.S. Department of Education.

Between 1985 and 1990, the cost of teen pregnancy was $120 billion, Tirozzi says. "We need to remind our leaders of the cost of not funding [prevention] programs."

For teens ages 18–19, the birth rate fell 10 percent from 1991 to 1997, says Barbara Broman, an official in the Office of Human Services Policy at the U.S. Department of Health and Human Services (HHS). For younger teens, the birth rate is down 16 percent.

The steepest decline, 23 percent, is reported for African-American teens, she says. The teen birth rate for Hispanics fell 7 percent.

Still, there are some disturbing trends, reports Melvin. For teens under 16, it's twice as likely that their first experience with sexual intercourse is non-voluntary. And for 40 percent of teenage girls, their first voluntary experience involves a partner who is more than three years older.

Tamara Kreinin, director of state and local affairs for the National Campaign to Prevent Teen Pregnancy, says 40 percent of pregnant teens are 17 or younger. And fewer teens are choosing abortion or adoption.

Shrinking Opportunities

Many of the presenters listed the negative consequences of teen pregnancy: Teens who get pregnant are less likely to graduate from high school, get a job, and go to college. They are more likely to be poor, go on welfare, and have used illegal drugs and alcohol.

Kreinin says teenagers most at risk of getting pregnant live in communities with high levels of poverty and high turnover, have sisters and peers who are pregnant, live in foster care or in an unstable household, have low expectations about their future, and are less successful in school.

"One of the biggest predictors of teen pregnancy is educational failure," she says. In many cases, students don't drop out because of pregnancy; they already were failing or were on the verge of dropping out, and pregnancy gave them an excuse to quit school.

The children of teen mothers tend to live in less supportive households, are more likely to do poorly in school, are more likely to be abused or neglected, and have a greater likelihood of becoming pregnant when they reach their teens. Kreinin says 70 percent of prisoners in the United States were children of teen mothers.

Types of Programs That Work

Tirozzi urges education leaders to "seek out programs with a track record of working somewhere."

Provide school-based health programs and services, he urges. Provide more counselors, psychologists, and social workers in the schools, and structure teen pregnancy prevention programs in the context of comprehensive child development, parenting, and health programs.

Broman says "a feeling of personal connection to home, family, and school is critical" to avoiding risky behavior.

HHS funds several programs at the state and local levels to address the problem. One of the largest is the $50 million Abstinence Only Education Program, enacted by Congress as part of welfare reform. It provides grants through the states for such activities as mentoring, counseling, and adult supervision.

The welfare reform law also attacks teen pregnancy by prohibiting assistance to any minor who is a custodial parent and who is not in school. And it requires unmarried teen parents to live with an adult, such as a parent or adult relative.

There is no data so far on whether abstinence-only programs are effective, notes Kreinin. But she says the research does show that "condom availability programs do not lead to increased sexual activity."

Broman says the most successful teen pregnancy programs are long-term. Education programs should provide basic, accurate information about the risks of sexual intercourse, advise youths on how to protect themselves, teach teens how to communicate with their peers, address social pressures, build teens' negotiation and refusal skills, and include teacher training.

For those engaged in outreach activities aimed at reducing teen pregnancy, Melvin offered the following advice: Accept that people have different values and agree to disagree to accomplish your goal, involve teens in your efforts, and focus on boys as well as girls.

"Preventing teen pregnancy is not quick and not cheap," says Kreinin. "We need to change teens' attitudes. Many believe pregnancy is okay. Young women who are pregnant say they love their child but wish they had delayed. We need to send out the message that 'adolescence is a time for education and growing up. Teen pregnancy is not okay.'"

The Effectiveness of the "Wait for Marriage" Message

Cheryl Wetzstein

In the following selection, *Washington Times* reporter Cheryl Wetzstein discusses the viability of promoting abstinence until marriage as a solution to teen pregnancies. She writes that some commentators believe teens are more willing to accept advice to wait for sex until they are married than to wait until some unspecified time in the future when they are "older" and "ready." According to these experts, Wetzstein states, the "wait for marriage" message can reduce the number of unwed teen pregnancies. Other experts, she notes, agree in theory but argue that it is difficult to sell a "wait for marriage" message to teens.

Three decades of teen-pregnancy prevention campaigns have scarcely dented the problem because "we have framed the problem falsely," author Maggie Gallagher says in a report released in September 1999.

"What we have called our 'teen-pregnancy' crisis is not really about teen-agers. Nor is it really about pregnancy. It is about the decline of marriage," says Mrs. Gallagher, director of the Marriage Project at the Institute for American Values in New York.

Waiting for marriage is the most powerful argument against teen pregnancy, but it has been drowned out by weaker messages, such as "wait until you're older" or "wait until you can afford a baby," says Mrs. Gallagher, a nationally syndicated columnist.

But "what are we telling young girls to wait for?" she asks.

"If the answer is 'another birthday,' how likely is it that a young woman who's passionately in love will say, 'No, no, I have to wait until I'm 20 to have sex with you?'" she says.

Young people who plan to marry, she explains, are more likely to be motivated to abstain from sex and avoid romantic relationships with unsuitable partners.

They are also more likely to use contraception and, should they have an unplanned pregnancy, place the baby for adoption with a married couple, she says in her report, "The Age of Unwed Mothers: Is Teen Pregnancy the Problem?"

If the country wants swifter reductions in unwed pregnancies, "the idea and ideal of marriage" has to be returned "to the center of our national discussion," she concludes.

Criticizing the Marriage Approach

Saving sex for marriage is a great idea, but too few kids want to hear it, say a chorus of teen-pregnancy prevention experts.

"Teens respond to messages about 'right now,'" says Marisa Nightingale, director of media programs at the National Campaign to Prevent Teen Pregnancy.

Recently, she says, the campaign asked some teens for 10 messages they would say to other teens to discourage pregnancy.

The most popular advice girls would give was "Sex won't make him yours and a baby won't make him stay," says Ms. Nightingale. Boys said they would tell peers that "You can always say 'no' even when you've said 'yes' before."

"Wait for marriage" didn't come up with either group, she recalled.

The national campaign has found that the most unifying message is that "adolescence is for education and growing up, not pregnancy and parenthood," says Sarah Brown, director of the privately funded campaign, which has the goal of reducing teen-pregnancy rates by a third by 2005.

"I'm in favor of marriage. I'm very happily married," says Mrs. Brown, who is also raising three teen-agers.

"But the notion that simply being married is the ticket" to solving the problem "misses the bigger picture," she says. Teen marriages that occur because the girl got pregnant are "notoriously unstable."

Kids Do Not Always Listen

Hal Donofrio, who handles dozens of abstinence-oriented media campaigns with the Baltimore-based Campaign For Our Children (CFOC), agrees that "wait until marriage," while admirable, is a hard message to sell to teens.

"I would suggest that 50 percent to even 75 percent of young people do not accept the wait-until-marriage message," he says, basing his estimate on 12 years of experience with teen media campaigns.

The CFOC has instead developed messages showing how abstinence leads to a better future, a better career, more self-esteem and better health, he says.

Other CFOC messages emphasize the perils of unwed parenthood, such as the costs of raising a baby and child support. "You play, you pay," warns one CFOC poster.

None of these messages spell out saving sex for marriage, Mr.

Donofrio says. Neither do they "preclude anyone from" reaching that conclusion, however, he adds.

The Family Life Educational Foundation in Philadelphia doesn't have "any problem selling this message," says John Stanton, a board member of the foundation. One of the group's most popular leaflets depicts sex as the wedding gifts a groom and bride give each other.

"Of course, like any other good message, kids don't listen every time," says Mr. Stanton. "But everyone—even this generation—relates to marriage because they know it's a commitment. They know the words are powerful and based on love and mutual respect."

"If you say 'wait until you're older,' what kind of advice is that?" Mr. Stanton says. "If you meet the girl of your dreams tonight . . . a boy could say, 'I did wait. I waited all day.'"

However, "We adults often underestimate the motivation within students to choose and vigorously hold to high ideals," says Richard Ross, an original leader of the True Love Waits campaign, which has spurred hundreds of thousands of teens to sign pledge cards saying they will defer sex until marriage.

Asking teens to simply postpone sex until some future date "has no power to move teen-agers to action," he says.

"I cannot imagine," adds Mr. Ross, who works with youth in Nashville, "that a grass-roots movement would have spread so rapidly through this generation of students if the call had simply been a challenge to 'wait just a little longer' to become sexually involved."

Mrs. Gallagher says she's not saying that the solution to teen unwed pregnancy is to "just marry them all off."

But "even early marriage is not a fate worse than unwed motherhood," says Mrs. Gallagher, a married mother who goes by her maiden name.

One of the basic problems with the current crop of teen-pregnancy prevention campaigns is that they tell teens to wait until they are older—and teens are doing just that.

As a result, the number of single mothers in their early 20s is growing, she says. Those who get pregnant as teens often choose to abort.

In 1997, for instance, birth data collected by the National Center for Health Statistics (NCHS) shows that unwed birthrates fell in every teen-age group, but rose among women aged 20–24.

Also, single women aged 20–24 had 438,632 babies in 1997. This was 52,830 babies more than all the teens combined.

The Thing Worth Waiting For

Why is the country "stone-cold silent" about the perils facing these unwed young-adult mothers? asks Mrs. Gallagher. Are the prospects "really that much different" for a 20-year-old mother than a 19-year-old single mother?

Why do young women think they are "old enough to be mothers, but too young to marry?" she asks.

The country needs more marriage education, marriage mentoring and marriage-building programs to highlight the emotional, and financial benefits of marriage, Mrs. Gallagher says. The "thing worth waiting for," she concludes, should be a good marriage and committed partner, "not just an 18th or 20th birthday."

Sex Education: Success or Failure?

Richard Nadler

Richard Nadler analyzes the effectiveness of school-based sex education in preventing teen pregnancy. According to Nadler, in past years advocates of sexual education argued that because teens would continue to have sex regardless, the best way to prevent teen pregnancy was to educate students about protection and make it easier for them to obtain contraceptives. However, he maintains, while this approach increased the rate of contraceptive use among teens, it also served to foster increased sexual activity. Instead, Nadler asserts, studies suggest that the recent drop in teen pregnancy rates is due to programs that stress abstinence. He also attributes the change to better morals and parental disapproval of adolescent sexual activity. Nadler is the editor of *K.C. Jones Monthly*, a midwestern journal of opinion.

For sex educators, the '90s were a decade of unrequited love. Academic research discredited their nostrums, and abstinence programs started to receive a respectful hearing. Then came the most crushing blow of all: Sexual activity among teenagers started to decline.

For years, sex-ed advocates had deflected criticism by explaining that teenagers were born to rut. Sure, the number of teenagers having sex was rising every year, in tandem with the expansion of sex education; and yes, these teenagers were having more sex, with more partners, at ever younger ages. But this, they contended, was an inexorable force of nature, and it was wiser to deal with the inevitable consequences than the inscrutable causes. "To do anything less than be explicit about protection is to stand by and let kids literally risk their lives," wrote one sex-ed advocate in 1993. It was an effective argument, recruiting to the cause of sex education and school-based condom distribution not just advocates of youthful sexual freedom but adults who, while perhaps disapproving, accepted parental impotence as a fact of modern life.

Now, however, the sexual revolution is receding among teens. At the start of the decade, adolescents were already registering higher rates of disapproval about teen sex than their elder brothers and sisters had. The ratio of teens with multiple partners fell, suggesting casual sex was on the decline. Deeper behavioral changes soon followed. Major social-science surveys recorded significant reductions in the percentage of sexually experienced teens. One study showed an 11 percent decline between 1991 and 1997. By 1996, teen rates of pregnancy, birth, and abortion had receded from their previous highs by 17 percent, 18 percent, and 37 percent respectively. The biggest improvements took place among younger teens. From 1988 to 1998, the National Survey of Adolescent Males recorded a 17 percent decrease in sexual experience among 15- to 17-year-old boys.

Sex Education the SIECUS Way

Confronted by what it once deemed impossible, the sex-ed establishment is taking a new tack. All this good news, they explain, proves they were right all along. Donna Shalala, the secretary of Health and Human Services, attributes the fall in teenage births to both increased abstinence and the "dramatic increase in contraceptive use at first intercourse." This is a bit like crediting both cigarettes and hoses for putting out a fire. Let's try to tease out cause and effect with more precision.

During the '70s and '80s, sex education became near-universal in the public schools. Most programs were based on a model developed by the Sexuality Information and Education Council of the United States (SIECUS). Under this model, school-based sex education had to be comprehensive so that kids could reach sensible decisions on sexual conduct. "Limiting the adolescent's tendency to explore, question, and ultimately come to his or her own conclusions stifles autonomy and a sense of self," wrote sex educators Susan Wilson and Catherine Sanderson. Shorn of ignorance and fear, kids can learn to enjoy sex without guilt or danger. A SIECUS expert recommended "teaching teens about oral sex and mutual masturbation in order to help them delay the onset of sexual intercourse."

Yet, according to this school of thought, detailed information is not so crucial for parents. "While it is generally desirable for parents to be involved in their children's contraceptive decisions," states a SIECUS position paper, "the right of each person to confidentiality and privacy . . . is paramount."

The results of this approach are now obvious, seen in the number of unplanned pregnancies, aborted fetuses, and welfare dependents. One SIECUS prediction, however, did prove correct: Sex ed increased the rate of contraceptive use among teens. But as teen "autonomy" trumped teen precaution, rates of sexual precocity rose even faster. While sex educators and the media obsessed over increased access to contraception, unwed teenaged girls were conceiving at record rates. Worse, the most rapid growth in sexual activity took place among the youngest teens. These teens use contraception erratically. The Centers for Disease Control reported that girls aged 15 to 17 were more than twice as likely to "miss" two or more birth-control pills per cycle as 18- and 19-year-olds.

So, can increased teen sexual activity fairly be attributed to sex ed? Yes, it can. Researchers have found that instruction in sexual biology and birth control is associated with earlier ages of first intercourse. When adults teach kids how to have sex, how to use contraceptives, and where to get them, the kids simply have more sex. And this approach is the heart and soul of sex-ed ideology.

For Carol Everett, who ran a chain of abortion clinics in the Dallas area, school-based programs were an investment. "When I went to those schools," she says, "my agenda was very clear. The first thing was to get the students to laugh at their parents, because if they laughed at their parents with me, they would not go home and tell their parents what I told them. . . . I'd say, 'Would your parents help you get on a method of contraception if you decided to become sexually active? Don't worry about that, here's a card, come to me.' And the next day . . . the telephone would start to ring." Everett, now a pro-lifer, says, "I knew that anytime I went to a school, the pregnancy rate went up sharply. I knew that by my own statistics. I knew that by working with Planned Parenthood, and by reading their statistics." More pregnancies meant more abortions.

Better Morals Have a Positive Effect

A 1993 study by Leighton Ku and others suggested that the most effective method in reducing teen sex activity is not comprehensive sex ed but the teaching of resistance (say-no-to-sex) skills. Another major study found that delayed sexual debuts are associated—surprise, surprise—with "high levels of parent-family connectedness [and] parental disapproval of their adolescent being sexually active." In perhaps the unkindest cut of all for the sex-ed establishment, the study noted that parents' "disapproval of their adolescent's using contraception" is "the strongest family variable counter indicative of teen pregnancy." Indeed, this disapproval is more protective against pregnancy than "effective contraceptive use [at] first/last sex." Other factors that have been found to delay intercourse include religious faith, an intact, two-parent household, a mother at home, and a "pledge of virginity."

This emerging portrait of effective sex education looks less like the SIECUS guidelines than like a Christian Coalition broadside: authoritative adults, buttressed by faith and moral absolutes, instilling in children pride in sexual purity and disapproval of promiscuity. Still another study found that the proportion of high-school girls learning resistance skills increased from 62 percent to 90 percent between the late '80s and 1995.

The final reason to doubt Shalala's contention that the decline in teen pregnancy can be attributed to a "dramatic increase in contraceptive use" is that, in fact, teen contraception has not become more effective in the '90s. Yes, condom use went up, but this was more than offset by the declining use of the birth-control pill. From 1988 to 1995, the percentage of currently sexually active 15- to 19-year-old females using the pill decreased from 59 to 45, while the percentage using male condoms increased from 33 to 37.

According to Contraceptive Technology, the authoritative source on contraceptive-failure rates, the typical user of birth-control pills has a 5 percent chance of getting pregnant over the course of a year; her chances rise to 14 percent if instead she relies on condoms. And condom awareness has done nothing to reduce the riskiest behaviors. The percentage of sexually active 15- to 19-year-olds using no contraception was 19 percent in 1988—and 19 percent in 1995.

In short, the big change among teens in the '90s has been not better contraception, but better morals. Fewer adolescents had intercourse, particularly those 17 years and younger. And those who did have intercourse had it less frequently, and with fewer partners. Less sex meant fewer pregnancies, births, and abortions.

TEACHING ABSTINENCE ONLY

Gary Thomas

In the following selection, Gary Thomas provides background on abstinence-only sexual education programs and the controversy surrounding them. The core of the controversy, he explains, is that the abstinence-only approach to sexual education does not include providing information about contraception. Some critics argue that because abstinence-only programs do not teach students about contraception, this approach cannot be useful in preventing teen pregnancy, Thomas writes. However, Thomas reports, abstinence-only programs have been employed successfully in various parts of the country. He describes in detail one such program that drastically lowered the teen pregnancy rate in Rhea County, Tennessee. Thomas is a freelance writer in Bellingham, Washington.

The call came at 11:30 P.M. on a Saturday night. "Miss Cathi," the teenage boy said, "I called you because I really need help. I really want to have sex, but I know I shouldn't."

Cathi Woods recognized his voice and knew the boy was calling from a "good Christian home." He had just returned from a date with his girlfriend and was terrified that their passion was getting out of hand.

"Both of us are Christians," the boy explained, "but we went too far. We didn't sleep together, but I'm worried about next time. You're the only person I can talk to."

Woods quietly walked the boy through an hour of phone counseling. "You know how bad you feel right now?" she asked.

"Yeah."

"If you go all the way, you'll feel a hundred times worse."

"I can't imagine feeling any worse than I do now," the young man confessed.

Woods proceeded to lead this young man through a litany of practical, real-life suggestions. By the end of the call, the boy was crying but extremely grateful.

"Thank you, Miss Cathi," he said. "You may have just saved my life."

Excerpted from Gary Thomas, "Where Love Waits," *Christianity Today*, March 1, 1999. Reprinted with permission from the author.

The Need for Abstinence Programs

Cathi Woods was the architect of what Rhea County (Tennessee) High School principal Pat Conner calls "a remarkably effective" abstinence program. In just one year, Rhea County dropped from being number one in teen pregnancies per capita in the state to tenth; during the second year, they dropped from tenth to forty-sixth and then, one year later, to sixty-fourth. Nothing else was done differently either in the school or the community, except for Woods's program. "I was quite surprised at the success," Conner admits. "Normally, one program doesn't have such an impact."

The program was so successful that when the state received federal money under a Title V federal grant, the entire $35,000 made available to Rhea County was awarded to Woods's program. Despite her outspoken Christian underpinnings, Woods was asked to spearhead an adolescent pregnancy council in Rhea County. Woods herself has since moved on to Boston to work with the Daybreak Pregnancy Resource Center, but the successful program she launched in Rhea County continues under the direction of her successor, Mona Coffield.

The need for such programs is acute. Although the rate of teen pregnancies has been decreasing in the 1990s, about one million teens become pregnant each year in the United States, according to the Medical Institute for Sexual Health; one-third of these pregnancies result in an abortion. Of the children carried to term, about 72 percent are born out of wedlock. This social devastation is exacerbated by an alarming health crisis among young people. In 1996, five of the top ten reportable infectious diseases—including the top four—were sexually transmitted. Adolescents (10–19) and young adults (20–24) are the age groups most at risk for acquiring a sexually transmitted disease (STD).

Local and federal governments have been throwing dollars at the problem without seeing much success. Every year, a staggering $10 billion is spent on fighting major STDs and their preventable complications, and this figure does not include AIDS-based programs.

Is it possible that a program that teaches abstinence is able to succeed where $10 billion has failed?

A Teenage Sexuality Crisis

Rhea County is home to Bryan College, named after the fiery William Jennings Bryan, best known for his defense of creationism during the famous Scopes trial. It is an extremely conservative county, where almost all identify themselves as Christian. Some might wonder: If Rhea County is so "religious," why did they have such a problem with premarital sexual activity?

Principal Conner offers a suggestion. "Some folks do not like the idea of discussing—sex. Some people think, 'If you don't talk about it, it doesn't exist.' That leaves an open door for young people." During their term as the state's worst problem area for teenage pregnancies, Rhea County used "Sex Respect," an abstinence curriculum used internationally. The program was very unpopular among the students, mostly because of the way it was taught.

"Kids thought it was a joke," Woods reports. Two of the oldest teachers in the school taught it, and neither teacher was entirely comfortable even mentioning the word sex, much less talking about the issues going through students' minds. What Cathi Woods was able to accomplish shows why programs alone will fail unless partnered with caring, capable people who dare to communicate with adolescents.

Woods, then director of the Women's Care Center, a local crisis-pregnancy facility, thought the problem could be addressed with a more straightforward approach where kids could ask anything and everything. She set out to schedule an appointment with the school superintendent. With the tenacity of a John Grisham heroine, she found out where the superintendent ate lunch, and then showed up for casual conversation over the course of several months. Having built a relationship, she soon had an appointment.

County executive Billy Ray Patton says he was ready to be approached. "I had sat on the school board for 13 years," he recalls, "and every year the teenage pregnancy rate kept getting higher and higher—almost 40 percent. We were racking our brains trying to find out what we could do to decrease this."

What Patton saw happening locally was also happening nationally—kids were becoming sexually active at an increasingly younger age. Lynn Bisbee of Care Net, a Christian prolife ministry, notes, "My focus when I first got started in abstinence education [1987] was in the high schools and at some colleges. But now, to be really effective, we have to reach students in junior high."

Congress has recognized the crisis of teenage sexuality as well as the relative failure of the "safe sex" approach and in 1997 appropriated new funds under a program called Title V, which distributes grants for abstinence-based education.

"Title V had a tremendous impact on the whole issue," Bisbee relates. "It turned the discussion into a national debate."

Straight Talking

In conservative Rhea County, Woods's Christian background was not an impediment. Administrators didn't fear Woods's faith so much as her intention to be very direct about sexual issues.

"I have to be direct," Woods explains, "because the kids aren't hearing about it in church." Conner remembers being extremely wary when approached about Woods's program. He expected tremendous negative reaction from people, most of whom would rather "sweep the problem under the rug" rather than face the fact that there was a serious problem of premarital sexual activity.

What won Conner over—or wore him out—was Woods's persistence. "She wouldn't let it die," Conner laughs. "Visits, calling, whatever it took." Neither Conner nor Patton felt Woods was simply after a job (she wasn't paid) or promoting a political agenda. Both felt confident that she wanted to reach out to kids. What Patton and Conner didn't realize is that Woods's concern was born out of personal travail.

As part of her preparation to develop her own program, Woods polled hundreds of sixth to ninth graders, asking them why they were having sex. Surprisingly, only one student answered "because I'm in love." Seventy-nine percent said they engaged in premarital sexual relations to "fit in or be cool." The second most popular answer—among males, not females—was "because it feels good." (Interestingly, not a single female chose this answer.)

Student Laura Cowden speculates that teens have sex because "they feel like they don't have any other choice. If they want to stay with whoever they're with, they have to go on to another level."

Rachel Held, another of Woods's students, points one finger at the media. Popular teen magazines such as *Seventeen* and *YM* teach "safe sex, safe sex, safe sex. They never even mention abstinence." These magazines are passed from student to student at school and greatly affect students' views.

Heidi Seera, a junior from a strong Christian home, suggests absent and overly permissive parents have something to do with kids becoming sexually active. "Some parents let their kids do whatever, and [they] hang around the wrong kids."

Influenced by a Fear of Disease

Part of Woods's appeal to the students was that she addressed them as a fellow struggler. At 36, Woods is attractive, gregarious—and a single mother. Her child was conceived before she became a Christian, and she freely shares her own battle to maintain sexual purity. "A woman in her midthirties is at her sexual peak," Woods told her students. "And my hormones are just as active as yours are."

This explains why it wasn't unusual for Woods to receive five calls a night, especially if she had recently been in the schools. Many began with, "Okay, Cathi, tell me what you do."

Because this program was for the public schools, Woods couldn't spout Bible verses. But Woods argued with pastors who suggested that abstinence doesn't work "without the Lord." "I beg to differ," she says firmly. "Non-Christian people get married as virgins all the time." Her approach was consistent with biblical values without using biblical arguments. . . .

Woods took an approach that worked for her even before she became a Christian—the fear of disease. "There are at least 25 sexually transmitted diseases out there," she points out. "When I started practicing abstinence, I did so out of fear of diseases. I was scared to death of what was out there, especially since I knew two people who died of AIDS. That was enough to make me say, 'Is sex worth it?' No."

When asked about this program, students most often remembered the section on STDs.

As Woods taught more and more on the dangers of a sexually promiscuous lifestyle, she realized that she needed to get tested herself. "I found out that my son's dad has hepatitis B, which is an incurable sexually transmitted disease. Now, I don't have it, but I could have gotten it. The woman you see standing before you could very well have contracted a fatal disease."

Woods had the students' attention when she described waiting for the results of her AIDS test. "You have to wait two weeks," she says. "I had a really good life, but when I thought back on all the 'good times,' I asked myself was it worth it if the good times had given me AIDS? No!"

Putting the Message Across

In addition to capitalizing on the kids' fear of disease, Woods was very honest about her own past failures and how they have affected her, particularly how her search for "father love" led her to get involved sexually before she was married. Heidi Seera said she felt Woods's personal struggles made the other students more willing to listen. "You knew that Cathi knew what she was talking about. She could put a lot of feeling into it."

While freshman Laura Cowden has chosen to remain abstinent, she knows of friends who were sexually active while going through Woods's program. "Cathi hit some heart strings. People I talked to who were sexually active said things like, 'Man, she understands how I feel about this, the pain and all the psychological consequences.'" Held says that "by the end of the class, people who were sexually active felt so dumb they wouldn't tell anybody," adding, "Now I can hold my head up high. Yeah, I'm a virgin."

Woods's program wasn't magical or even particularly unusual. One of the factors working in her favor was Rhea County's willingness to give her two weeks. Often schools will limit the presentation to three days (one hour a day).

Day one begins with Woods's personal experience. Cowden calls this the most helpful part of Woods's program. The classroom usually becomes absolutely silent when Woods says, "If God came up to me and said, 'Cathi, I'll give you one wish in the entire world; what is it?' My one wish would be that I could be a virgin again. I can't think of anything more wonderful than being a virgin on my wedding night."

During the second and third days of the program, Woods discusses the practical nature of sexual progression and the personality differences between men and women. Woods also asks students to describe their "ideal" mate. Students are often shocked when they hear other known-to-be sexually active students proclaim, "I want to marry a virgin." "At least 75 percent of the students include this in their profile," Woods says, "and it really opens up the other students' eyes."

Kids Want Boundaries

During the next few days, Woods splits the boys from the girls and discusses Dr. Joe McIlhaney's slides on STDs and other topics such as puberty and pregnancy. Day eight is a discussion of AIDS and the showing of Focus on the Family's Sex, Lies, and the Truth video.

The ninth day includes a discussion of individual goals and dreams. Students are encouraged to consider where they want to be one, five, and ten years from now. Woods also uses several games to emphasize the consequences of premarital sex.

Day ten is left open for the students to ask Woods any question that may have been left unanswered. The questions are written on cards so the students can ask them anonymously. This is where earlier abstinence teachers often failed, as the questions can get personal and embarrassing. Seera says Woods "was loose and didn't seem embarrassed one bit, and that really helped open up the class."

While Woods is clear that no question is out of bounds, she is also outspoken that sexual activity outside of marriage is harmful. This no-exceptions approach doesn't appear to turn most students off. Woods has found that "kids are hungry for boundaries."

Woods's abstinence program, though successful, was not without its difficult days. Woods recalls one afternoon when the class was being unusually rowdy. The kids whooped and hollered and laughed about every innuendo in the discussion. It was getting out of hand when she finally stopped and said, "You know, guys, I don't get paid a dime for doing this, but I do it because I know if I can change one person and keep one person from making the same mistakes I did, it'll be worth it."

Woods turned back to the blackboard to hide her tears, and at that moment the bell rang. She let the students file out, still turned toward the blackboard, when she felt a tap on her shoulder. Woods turned and saw one of the school "jocks," a very popular, athletic male, who said, "Miss Cathi, you've already changed my life.". . .

No Guarantee of Success

Her relationships with these kids made it extremely difficult for Woods to leave Rhea County. "I still feel so connected to those kids," she says. Even though she has been gone for several months, she still gets long-distance phone calls late on Friday and Saturday nights. This is a thing of wonder for Woods. "Here I am, an old, middle-aged woman, and these kids want to talk to me!"

Though the results of Woods's program were dramatic, working with teens virtually guarantees less than perfect success. Woods recalls a young girl who started dating when she was just 14 years old. Her boyfriend was pressuring her to have sex, and the young girl occasionally called Woods with updates.

"He said he'll leave me if I don't have sex with him soon."

"Then he doesn't love you," Woods tried to convince her.

These calls went on for months, until late one night, Woods received another desperate call. "I finally gave in a couple weeks ago." There was a long pause. "And now I'm late."

Woods urged her to come in and get a pregnancy test. As soon as her boyfriend had found out she was late, he left her. The pregnancy test was positive, so Woods referred her to a doctor, which yielded an even more devastating revelation. In that one sexual encounter the young girl not only became pregnant, she also contracted herpes, which she will now have to live with for the rest of her life.

Safe Sex Versus No Sex

Despite its success, Woods's abstinence-only approach is controversial. Many groups, including Planned Parenthood, argue that abstinence should be presented as an option, but that teens should also be instructed about the proper use of contraceptives. Most of these programs also work toward providing free contraceptives, especially condoms.

Congressional passage of Title V may have swung the debate more toward the abstinence side. "When we first started talking about abstinence," Bisbee relates, "the safe-sex proponents downplayed and dismissed it, thinking we were unrealistic asking kids to be sexually abstinent. Some even said it was dangerous."

In April of 1998, the fight over contraceptive or abstinence-only sex education broke out anew after a study suggested that students who have access to free condoms at school are no more sexually active than those who don't. The L.A. County study was published in Family Planning Perspectives by the Alan Guttmacher Institute (the research arm of Planned Parenthood). . . .

The National Coalition for Abstinence Education (NCAE) immediately countered that "this study is not honest research—it is number twisting for the exclusive purpose of asking for more tax funding.". . .

Woods explains her commitment to abstinence-only programs this way: "Even if you ignore the fact that there are at least 25 active sexually transmitted diseases out there, and even if you ignore teen pregnancy, you can't take out the fact that every time you have sex with someone and they leave you, there's a broken heart. These girls are struggling with a broken heart, crying in my office, and that's the time I tell them, 'Do you want to be here again?'

"I suffer from a broken heart because of this," Woods confesses.

"The true empowerment of women is teaching abstinence, because abstinence gives women control of their bodies."

The teens interviewed for this article were unanimous in their opinion that sex education should be taught in the schools. "Especially the abstinence," Held added, "because I'm really tired of this safe sex stuff."

Seeking Solutions: How Best to Teach Sexuality

Susan Okie

Susan Okie, a health writer for the *Washington Post*, addresses the issue of the most effective way to encourage sexual abstinence and prevent teen pregnancies. According to Okie, teens' decisions about whether and when to become sexually active hinge primarily on their relationship with their parents, their religious or moral values, and their socioeconomic status. Most educators and experts agree that open communication between parents and their children is key to helping teens make a wise choice, she notes. Parents and schools both have important roles to play in sexuality education, she writes: Schools teach important information about sexuality, while parents impart personal and family values. Okie also reports that there is no conclusive proof that sex education programs encourage increased sexual activity among teens.

Spring sunshine lights up blank sheets of paper as six kids, aged 9 through 11, from Baltimore's Latrobe housing project grasp their pencils and get ready to draw their futures.

In a moment, the pencils begin to fly.

"I want to be a famous book writer for children's books," says Jasmine Bell.

"I want to be a lawyer," says Thion Grant.

"I want to go out in space. Then I want to get married," says Christopher Jones.

University of Maryland health educators Yvonne Summers, George Cornick and Jennifer Galbraith listen, smile and applaud those dreams. Then they shuffle a pack of cards and deal out some alternative fortunes.

"These are called adjustments to your future," they tell the children. "These are things that could go wrong and you have to figure out what you're going to do."

One card says, "You have tested positive for HIV." Another reads, "You got a girl pregnant."

The kids' faces fall as they consider how such events might hobble their progress toward their goals. They discuss what they can do to keep them from happening.

"Use a condom," says Christopher. "Take those birthday pills."

"Don't have sex," suggest two other boys.

Cornick seizes on that response. "Don't have sex, that's correct," he says. "It looks like having sex when you're a teenager, or when you're too young, sets you up for a lot of trouble in the future."

Abstinence Versus Safe Sex

Don't have sex. Use a condom. Ever since the nation began to grapple with the AIDS epidemic in the mid-1980s, the issue of sex education for children and teens has acquired a life-and-death urgency. Multiple polls indicate that most Americans want schools to teach their kids what they need to know to avoid pregnancy and prevent sexually transmitted infections. At the same time, many adults worry about how best to transmit their own values to their children. The generation that once cautioned "Don't trust anyone over 30" are now parents themselves, and many are finding it as difficult as their own parents did to talk to their kids about sex, love and relationships.

"We had this cry from parents," said Bonita F. Stanton, a University of Maryland pediatrician who did community surveys in Baltimore before designing Focus on Kids, the program now underway at the Latrobe housing project and other sites. "They thought they were being inadequate, but they had no idea how to talk and what kinds of rules they should set."

The national debate over what children should be taught in sex education courses has been boiled down, in media reports and in many people's minds, to "abstinence versus condoms."

Many educators say the fight over abstinence versus condoms vastly oversimplifies the issue of how to provide children with truly comprehensive sexuality education. They argue that as children grow up, they need to be part of broad, age-appropriate discussions about gender roles, sexuality, communication and values that involve parents, schools, churches, the media and other sectors of society.

"Kids today learn about sex from here, there and everywhere," said Deborah M. Roffman, who has worked as a sexuality educator in Maryland for 27 years. "Openness in the news media about sexual topics is a real boon to our kids. They have a different baseline."

But that new societal openness doesn't necessarily mean that most children are getting what they need to become sexually responsible adults. Studies have shown that, while information is important, the quality of parent-child relationships, religious or moral values, socioeconomic status and family stability are critical determinants of children's decisions about whether and when to become sexually active.

Roffman and other educators said parents frequently overestimate how much their children learn about sexuality in school and how effective a sex education course, by itself, is likely to be in influencing their future behavior.

"Only 5 percent of young people receive anything like a comprehensive sexuality education program," said Debra W. Haffner, president of the Sexuality Information and Education Council of the United States (SIECUS).

SIECUS lists 36 topics that it considers part of such a comprehensive program. About 93 percent of U.S. high schools offer sexuality programs with information about the human immunodeficiency virus that causes AIDS, and the majority include information about puberty, abstinence, contraception, pregnancy and sexually transmitted diseases (especially AIDS). However, many programs tend to avoid certain other topics—particularly masturbation, abortion and homosexuality—which SIECUS recommends be covered.

Haffner said when she teaches eighth-graders about sexuality at her church's Sunday school, parents sometimes say to her, "Thank you for what you're giving my child for life." She said she tells them, "You can't do these programs as an immunization. I can give them what they need in the eighth grade. I can't prepare them to be 16 and in love—or 40 and in a 20-year-old marriage."

The Effects of Programs Vary

Yet studies suggest that some sexuality education programs can influence adolescents' behavior. During the 1990s, largely because of the AIDS epidemic, scientists have begun a concerted effort to evaluate how different types of educational programs affect children's actions— for example, whether kids who participate are less likely to have sex or more likely to use condoms. Such studies were partly prompted by the fear that providing information about condoms and birth control might actually increase sexual activity, especially among teenagers.

A wealth of studies now indicate that fear is unfounded. "The overwhelming weight of evidence indicates that sex education programs do not hasten the onset of sexual debut," says Brian L. Wilcox, a professor of psychology at the University of Nebraska-Lincoln who has reviewed the research. Nor do such programs increase the frequency of intercourse, the number of partners, teen pregnancy rates or the incidence of sexually transmitted diseases.

Indeed, recent statistics suggest that many teenagers are heeding messages about abstinence, birth control and condoms. The proportion of 15-to-19-year-old girls who are sexually active fell from 53 percent in 1988 to 50 percent in 1995. For boys in the same age group, the proportion fell from 60 percent to 56 percent. The percentage of 15-to-19-year-olds who reported using condoms the first time they had sex tripled between 1975 and 1995 (from 18 percent to 54 percent). The teen pregnancy rate has dropped in the past two decades, from 247 pregnancies per 1,000 sexually active teens in 1974 to 210 in 1994.

Just how much sex education programs may be contributing to these favorable trends isn't clear. Five educational programs, the newest of which is the University of Maryland's Focus on Kids, have been identified by the federal Centers for Disease Control and Prevention (CDC) as effective in HIV prevention because they have been shown to delay sexual initiation or increase condom use, based on the findings of well-designed scientific studies published in peer-reviewed journals. However, even these programs seem to have only "modest effects" on behavior, Wilcox said.

"They work with some teens but not all teens," he said. "Almost none has been replicated in different sites. They don't necessarily translate to different cultures and geographic contexts."

Scrutinizing a Program's Effectiveness

A teenager's decision about whether to have sex—and whether to use condoms or birth control—depends not just on what that child knows but also on a host of other factors, including self-esteem, communication and refusal skills, family and cultural attitudes about sex and childbearing, and access to contraception. Most sexuality education programs address only part of that mix.

"We have no Cadillac programs out there," said Wilcox. "We have a few Hondas. But mainly what we've got out there are Yugos, and the Yugos don't work well."

Federal lawmakers recently addressed the situation. In 1996, as part of the welfare reform law, Congress appropriated $50 million annually for five years that states could use to fund sex education programs that teach "abstinence only" until marriage. Funding began in 1998, and all states have applied for and accepted the federal money. It can't be used for programs that also discuss birth control and ways that sexually active teenagers can avoid sexually transmitted diseases. Despite this federal funding, few of the programs focusing on "abstinence only" have undergone careful scientific scrutiny to determine whether they're effective, Wilcox said.

In May 1998, for the first time, researchers reported a significant, although short-lived, effect on adolescent sexual behavior from an abstinence-only program evaluated according to a strict research design known as a randomized controlled trial. The study by Princeton psychology professor John B. Jemmott and two colleagues is one of the few that have tested such a program in this type of trial, which scientists consider the most bias-free method for comparing different treatments or interventions.

In the study, published in the May 19, 1998, *Journal of the American Medical Association,* 659 African American students from three Philadelphia middle schools were randomly assigned to one of three programs:

one that focused on abstinence, one that focused on "safer" sex and condoms, and one (the "control" group) that discussed health promotion without focusing on sexual behavior. Each program contained eight one-hour classes and took place on two consecutive Saturdays.

More Work Is Needed

When participants were surveyed three months after the programs ended, those in the abstinence program were significantly less likely than those in the control group to report having had sexual intercourse. But that difference had disappeared when participants were surveyed again six months and 12 months after completing the program.

In contrast, the safer-sex group reported more frequent condom use than did the control group when surveyed at three, six and 12 months.

Jemmott said it may simply be more difficult to persuade adolescents to be sexually abstinent than to use condoms. "One possibility is that there's more external pressure to have sex than there is external pressure not to use condoms," he said.

Wilcox said one of the largest scientific tests of an abstinence-only program was a California study, published in 1997, of a curriculum called Postponing Sexual Involvement (PSI), a five-session program for seventh- and eighth-graders. In that study, 10,600 students were randomly assigned to receive either their regular health education classes or to receive the regular classes plus PSI. Study participants were surveyed three months and 17 months after the program ended. Children who had participated in PSI were just as likely as those who had not to have become sexually active, to have become pregnant or to have gotten a sexually transmitted disease.

Jemmott said researchers have much to learn about how to make abstinence-only programs effective. "I would say there's been a lot more research on safer-sex interventions than on abstinence interventions," he said. "There needs to be more work in developing abstinence interventions so that we can learn how to sustain the effects."

The Need for a Clear Message

Douglas Kirby, a senior research scientist at California's ETR Associates and an expert on sex education curricula, noted that the more elaborate and comprehensive programs advocated by SIECUS haven't been thoroughly evaluated either. The few studies of such programs in the early 1980s suggested they increased teenagers' knowledge but didn't appear to reduce sexual activity. However, educators have learned a considerable amount since then about what components make a program likely to work. "Values neutral" programs that leave it up to kids to figure out what's best for themselves have not been found as effective in changing behavior as programs that take a clear position.

Research shows that the most effective programs share several key characteristics. For instance, Kirby said, all five programs that have been found by the Centers for Disease Control (CDC) to change kids' behavior focus clearly on reducing one or more behaviors that can lead to pregnancy or HIV infection. To get their point across, they incorporate a variety of teaching methods and materials, appropriate to the participants' age, culture and sexual experience. They also are based on recognized theories of behavior change that have been found effective in other settings.

They provide accurate information about the risks of unprotected sex and how to avoid those risks. They address social pressures that adolescents often face in relation to sex. They provide practice in communication and refusal skills, and take enough time to allow participants to complete the activities. And they are taught by trained teachers or peers who believe in the program.

"They give a clear message," said Kirby. "One may be, wait till you're older to have sex. Another may be, always use condoms when you have sex. Those are clear messages for different target groups. Every activity is designed to reinforce that message."

For example, during a single classroom session at the Latrobe housing project, kids first discussed their goals and how pregnancy, HIV infection or drug abuse might affect them. Then they talked about the steps they'd go through when making a tough decision and where they could turn for help.

They did a role-playing exercise in which they practiced asking a teacher for an appointment to talk about a problem. They made lists of places where they could seek information: a dictionary, a library, a hospital, a telephone book. Each then used the telephone to call an AIDS hot line and ask how the disease is transmitted. They played a game called "Human Knot," in which they linked hands, tangled themselves up, and had to disentangle each other by working together, without letting go.

Each part of the session provided not only information, but practice in communicating and coping.

"Sometimes, kids don't seem like they're listening, but if you put information in their heads . . . somewhere, down the line, you'll connect," said Cornick, who has worked with the Focus on Kids program for about two years.

Reducing Risky Behavior

Stanton, the University of Maryland pediatrician, designed Focus on Kids for African American children between the ages of 9 and 15 after community surveys in inner-city Baltimore showed that 40 percent of kids in that age group were sexually experienced. Parents identified their adolescents' risk of HIV infection as a major concern.

"Here, the initial sexual involvement is intercourse," Stanton said. "There isn't the period of a couple of years of light petting [followed by] heavy petting" first. The program seeks to get kids to postpone having intercourse until they are more mature and better able to plan and make decisions. "The older we can get kids before they engage in sex," the better, Stanton said.

Two other programs found effective by the CDC, "Be Proud! Be Responsible!" and "Becoming a Responsible Teen," were also developed to target African American youth. Two additional programs, "Reducing the Risk" and "Get Real About AIDS," were developed and tested in ethnically mixed populations in high schools in California and Colorado.

The CDC's Division of Adolescent and School Health identifies and helps disseminate effective curricula for reducing risky sexual behavior among adolescents as part of its Research to Classroom project, said Janet Collins, the division's branch chief. The idea is to find innovative, broadly applicable curricula that an average teacher can use and make them readily available to everyone.

"We package them, we train [teachers], we make them visible," Collins said. But it's up to local school districts to decide what kind of programs to adopt.

Shared Responsibilities

In the Washington area, policies on sexuality education in schools vary among local jurisdictions. But whatever the policy on the books, teachers have to be comfortable discussing sexuality for a program to be effective, said Barbara K. Huberman, director of training and sex education for Advocates for Youth, a Washington-based nonprofit organization. That usually requires training.

"You can have the most fabulous curriculum in the world," she said. "It will go into the drawer because that particular teacher is fearful, concerned about parental reaction or not comfortable dealing with these issues."

Roffman, the Baltimore sexuality educator, said parents and schools both have vital roles to play in teaching children about sexuality. "Parents have teachable moments that are crucially important, that come up as often as you look for them," she said. "As a child's parent, I am the only person who can tell my child what I think and value."

Schools, on the other hand, have methodology. "They have trained teachers, curricula, resources . . . and groups of peers who can be utilized, in the safety of a well-run sexuality course, to tell the truth to one another, to support one another," Roffman said.

At a recent session of Roffman's seventh-grade human sexuality course at the Park School, a private school in the Baltimore suburb of Brooklandville, that kind of communication was evident. Kids were asked to pair off and take turns telling each other (or a reporter who participated in the class) what they thought about issues like homosexuality, gender stereotypes and dating.

They had plenty to say. Catherine Rosen and Alina Odnopozova said they thought homosexuality was "totally normal" for some people. Josh Lauren said he found it easy to talk about sex with his dad. Michael Schaffer said he didn't like the ways people stereotype girls and boys, because "they fit for some people but not for everybody."

Roffman believes learning to communicate is at the core of becoming comfortable with sexuality throughout life. She said students in her high school classes are required to read two newspapers a day and discuss "all the sex articles" except the ones dealing with crimes and scandals. In the last few months they've talked about Viagra, the Iowa septuplets and the Supreme Court decision on a same-sex sexual harassment case.

"I have a rather simple philosophy," she said. "Those things you communicate well about, you handle well.". . .

Parental Supervision and Strong Values

When it comes to teenagers and sex, good parenting makes a big difference. For all the debate over sex education in schools, the evidence so far suggests that parents play a stronger role than school-based educational programs in encouraging sexual abstinence and preventing teen pregnancies.

Studies show that close parent-child relationships, close parental supervision and strong religious or moral values all reduce the chances that a teenager will have sex or become pregnant.

But many parents find it hard to talk to their kids about sex. Some worry that if they urge their adolescent not to have intercourse, yet also bring up condoms and contraception, they'll be sending a mixed message.

"It's hard for parents to tread the line of, 'When am I pushing sex?'" said Stanton. "It's a tough one."

The best way to make parent-child discussions about sex comfortable is not to treat the topic as unusual, said Kirby. Age-appropriate conversations about sex, love and relationships should start in childhood and continue throughout adolescence.

"You don't have a single conversation but multiple conversations," Kirby said. "Sex should be like lots of other topics—you discuss it for 20 seconds, then move on. You don't wait for kids to ask you questions, because they will get the message that this is something you don't talk about."

Haffner agreed with that approach. "If you want to talk to your teenager, you'd better be talking to your 4-year-old," she said. "For some kids, you will wait your whole life for them to ask a question. We don't wait for our children to ask to teach them how to cross the street."

Parents should listen to their child, but not hesitate to express their own values, Kirby suggests. "It's a good idea for parents to express their values about when and under what conditions young people should engage in sex—and to express their views about contraception," he said.

Parents Do Know More

One easy way to initiate a conversation about love, sex and values is to discuss the characters in a movie or television show. Haffner allows her 12-year-old daughter to watch the evening soap opera *Dawson's Creek,* but only if Haffner watches it with her. After each episode, they discuss the characters' relationships and behavior. She said her daughter doesn't usually find much to emulate.

Haffner said fear of giving mixed messages shouldn't deter parents. "We give mixed messages all the time," she said. For example, parents often tell their teenagers they shouldn't drink, but also warn them that if they do drink, not to drive.

"It's important to communicate your family's values" about sex to your children, Haffner said. "The next part of the message is, 'If you are starting to think about having intercourse, I hope you will come and talk to me.'"

The third part should be, "It is critical that if you have intercourse, that you protect yourself by using contraception and condoms," she added.

Many parents complain that teens think they know all about sex already. But that's not what teenagers think, a survey suggests. In a nationally representative survey conducted in April 1998 for the National Campaign to Prevent Teen Pregnancy, only 6 percent of adolescents aged 12 to 17 thought they knew as much or more than their parents about sex and relationships. Topics that the teenagers wished their parents would talk more about included sexually transmitted diseases and birth control, how to manage dating and relationships, and knowing how and when to say "no."

CHAPTER 3

MAKING TOUGH CHOICES

A Pregnant Teen's Options

Robert W. Buckingham and Mary P. Derby

Robert W. Buckingham is a professor of public health at New Mexico State University in Las Cruces and the author of numerous books. Mary P. Derby is a maternal child health clinical nurse specialist at Harvard Pilgrim Health Care in Boston, Massachusetts. The following selection is excerpted from their book *"I'm Pregnant, Now What Do I Do?"* Buckingham and Derby focus on options available today to pregnant teens—to continue or end their pregnancy, to raise their child, or to give up the child for adoption. These options, they explain, are among the legal rights of pregnant teens, although in some instances parental consent may be required. Buckingham and Derby recount the reasons why some teens opt for abortion or adoption and describe the emotional cost of each. Teens who choose to keep their babies often face economic and social hardship as well, the authors note. They stress that even though teens have a greater number of options and more freedom currently than they did in the past, they also have greater responsibility.

Pregnancy is a major event in any woman's life, but especially in a young woman's life because so many areas of her life aren't settled yet. When most teens become pregnant they are still in school and financially dependent on a parent or guardian. Many teens are developing interests, and deciding what they want out of life. Making a decision about a pregnancy is a major event, especially at this stage in your life. Each option has its advantages and disadvantages. Each option brings with it a personal benefit or gain for you, as well as a personal loss. *No matter which option you choose, you can't escape a loss.* You will feel some pain from your loss and it will be necessary for you to grieve. Deciding when and whether to have a baby is a very personal decision. Only you know which option is best for you. The benefits and losses for each option will have a different meaning for each young woman. . . .

Minors Have Legal Rights

Each option you have is a legal option. Legally you can choose to continue your pregnancy and raise your child, or you can place your child for adoption. Legally you can also choose to terminate your pregnancy. Many young women aren't aware of their legal rights. They don't realize they can get a pregnancy test, seek pregnancy counseling, have an abortion, or get prenatal care without informing their parents. This is a sensitive issue for some young women. They need to know their confidentiality will be maintained before they will seek care.

If you are a minor (under age eighteen) and living with your parents, your parents are responsible for you. As part of their responsibility, your parents' consent is required in most cases whenever you receive medical care and treatment. Parental consent laws vary in each state. In some states your health care provider may be required to inform one or both of your parents, and in other states one or both parents' consent is needed before medical care can be provided to you. However, there are times when your parents' notification or consent is not required.

Laws relating to health care for minors vary from state to state. Almost every state allows a minor to consent to the diagnosis and treatment of a sexually transmitted disease, as well as purchase non-prescription contraceptives, such as condoms. Most states also allow minors to consent to pregnancy-related care, which includes family planning and contraceptive services, prenatal care, delivery, and care after delivery.

As a minor, you can also get family planning services in federally funded programs without your parents' notification or consent. However, these programs are mandated to encourage parental involvement. This means these providers will encourage you to notify your parents and they may offer to speak to your parents with you. They will not do this unless they have your permission first, though. This is a difficult issue for some teens to talk to their parents about, and some teens appreciate their health care provider's support.

You have the legal right to an abortion; however, most states have parental notification or consent laws. . . .

Raising a Baby Is Hard Work

About half of the young women who become pregnant each year choose to raise their baby. You can raise your baby on your own or with the help and support of your family, your boyfriend, and/or others. You and your boyfriend can also marry, but few teens today choose to do this. According to statistics, of the teens who do marry, more than half of their marriages end in divorce.

Raising a baby is an awesome responsibility, even for women who are older when they become mothers. The lack of life experience, education, and financial security among teenagers makes it even harder for them to raise their children. Each teen parent has a different experience. Some teens meet the responsibility and challenge of parenting with strength and determination. Other teens become frustrated and overwhelmed with parenting. Lots of teens wished they had postponed parenting. As teen mother Sharon said:

> I love my daughter, yet there are times when I wish I had waited to have my baby. There is so much responsibility. There are so many things I worry about. There's never enough time in the day for me to do everything I need to do. I rush all day long. It begins early in the morning when I race around to get us both ready for school, and it seems like it never ends, especially on the nights when she doesn't sleep well.

Another teen, Kathy, said: "My son is great. I enjoy being a mother. I'm a good mother. I didn't know there was so much you had to do. Sometimes I think I would have been better off if I had put off having kids for a while. I grew up too fast. There are days when I feel so old, and I'm still just a kid."

Having a baby will drastically change your life. You will experience losses in many areas of your life. Your relationships will change with your family, your boyfriend, and other friends. You may have difficulty completing your education and you will probably struggle financially to make ends meet. Teen parenting has been linked with poverty. Teen moms do eventually catch up, but it takes them a very long time, and they will only make one-half the family income of their peers who postponed childbearing until their mid-twenties or later.

Abortion and Adoption Are Options

About one-third of all teens who become pregnant each year choose to terminate their pregnancy. For most teens, abortion is a personal, complex decision. Many teens carefully balance their religious or moral beliefs with their other needs when making their decision. Some women choose abortion even though it conflicts with their religious beliefs because they feel it is the best option for themselves. Other women don't choose abortion, either because they waited too long and it was no longer a possibility, or they can't resolve their religious or moral beliefs. There is an emotional loss associated with abortion. For each woman the emotional loss is different. As Jessica said:

> I'm not happy with myself that I had an abortion. It's against my religious views. But at the time there was too much going against me in my life. I felt I did the responsible thing. It would have been too emotionally traumatic for me at that time to bring a child into this world.

Monica chose to place her baby for adoption because she felt she wasn't ready to be a parent at the time and because she was morally opposed to abortion. Monica says:

> Abortion was never an option for me. I don't believe in abortion, although I wouldn't discourage another woman from having one if that's what she thought was best for her. I worked through the pros and cons of parenting versus adoption. For two months I wrote down how I felt about each option. Even though in the back of my mind I knew adoption was right for me, going through the process was very helpful. It made it concrete in my mind. It became very clear to me that adoption was the best decision I could make for my baby and myself.

Adoption is an option for a young woman, such as Monica, who feels she's not ready emotionally or financially to raise a child, and who does not feel comfortable terminating her pregnancy. There are many individuals and couples today who want to fulfill their dream of being parents. Adoptive children are raised in loving families. Some young teens do not choose adoption because they are worried that the emotional loss they would experience would be too great. A young woman who chooses adoption does experience the loss of parenting her baby. However, for the young women who choose adoption, this loss is not as great to them as the loss they believe they would have experienced if they had chosen either parenting or abortion. They want what's best for their baby, and they are concerned that at that point in their life they cannot be a good parent. Both Monica and Carolyn felt adoption was their best option. They are happy with their decision and do not have regrets. As Carolyn said:

> I didn't want to have in abortion. . . . I could have raised my child with my parents' support. But that wasn't what I wanted to do. I felt it wasn't fair for my child to grow up without a father. I wanted my child to have a better life than what I was able to give. I knew it would be hard for me to get my education. I wasn't emotionally ready to be a parent. The more I thought about it, adoption made the most sense.

Times Have Changed

Teen sex and teen pregnancy are not new. However, sexual activity begins at an earlier age for more young teens today than it did years ago. According to the Alan Guttmacher Institute, about 50 percent of the young women and 75 percent of the young men today have sex before age eighteen, compared to 35 percent of young women and 55 percent of young men in the early 1970s. Young men and women also marry three to four years later today than teens did decades ago. In the past young teens did get pregnant outside of marriage, but it was handled much differently.

In the 1950s through the early 1970s when a young woman became pregnant she either married the man or secret arrangements were made to place her baby for adoption. Abortion was not legal until 1973. If a young woman wanted an abortion, she had to have an illegal one. Illegal abortions were associated with serious health risks. Some women died from them, and some women suffered serious medical complications. Fewer single women at that time raised their children alone. Society expected a young woman to marry or place her baby for adoption. Single women who raised their children were viewed as being less stable and more emotionally needy than the young women who placed their babies for adoption. There was a stigma attached to single parenting. It was considered socially unacceptable to be a young, single mother. Public assistance did not exist then for women who needed financial support so that they could stay at home to raise their children. Mosella was a single teenager when she became pregnant in 1955. She shares her experience so you can understand what women experienced in previous years:

> I was single and a teenager in 1955 when I became pregnant. That was over forty years ago and times have certainly changed since then. Back then, sex was only for married couples. It was something that happened behind closed doors. No one talked about sexuality. That was taboo. There was no sex education. It was almost impossible to get birth control. Women did not have careers; they married and had babies.
>
> If you were single and got pregnant your options were limited and bleak. You were expected to marry the father of your baby. Some women placed their babies for adoption and other women had illegal abortions. It didn't matter which option you chose. They were equally traumatic. If you planned to marry the man or to place your baby for adoption, you had to involve your family. This meant acknowledging to your family that you had had premarital sex. You got caught doing something you weren't supposed to do. You were ashamed and felt guilty to have to tell or burden your family. You risked rejection by them and by society.
>
> I never meant to get pregnant. I got caught. I felt very sad and guilty about my pregnancy. I didn't have anyone to talk to. There was no one I could trust. I was brought up in a strict family. My dad died when I was young. My brothers were brought up to be the head of the household. I couldn't face telling my family, so I made my decision alone.
>
> At the time I got pregnant, I was one of the few colored

women attending a prominent music conservatory. I had worked very hard to be accepted to that school. I was awarded a full scholarship to attend. . . . That was something I was extremely proud of. My family and friends were also proud of me, and they had high hopes for me. I felt I couldn't disappoint them. I couldn't marry the father of my baby, and I couldn't place my baby for adoption. They did not have the type of adoption arrangements back then that they do today. My other two choices were to raise my baby alone or to have an abortion. I couldn't see bringing a child into this world. There weren't any good jobs then. I didn't know how I could manage, how I could be a good parent under those circumstances. My child would have lived in poverty, and that was not an option for me. I was determined to have a better life. Sure, I was spoiled. I wanted a taste of life. I wanted to experience life. It was not my mission to be a wife and mother. I was a dreamer. I had been given a chance of a lifetime. To be a colored woman attending a music conservatory was a very big opportunity for me. I wanted to fulfill a life dream. I wanted a career in music.

I chose to have an abortion. At first I tried to miscarry. But then I realized I didn't want to sacrifice my health. So I went out of town and had an abortion. I was very fortunate, my physical health was not harmed in any way. But I hurt emotionally. I'm Catholic, and so I felt very guilty about what I had done. For years, it was very hard for me to deal with because of my religion and also because I did everything alone. I never told anyone, so I suffered in silence. Twenty years later I finally told my family.

Who's to know whether I did the right thing? Who's to say? I feel I did the best thing for myself, and that's what counts. No one can judge me. I have healed since then. My faith in myself and in God saved me. Along the way I found help. Friends mentored me, they took an interest in me, they helped me reach my potential. I shared my feelings with a therapist. That also helped a lot. I've traveled to many places. I've lived a very rich and rewarding life. I have my master's degree in education and I have a career in music. I've fulfilled my dreams.

My advice to other teens is to trust someone. It's a big decision to make. Don't go through the decision process alone, like I did. Get proper counseling. No matter what you choose to do, take good care of your health. Today you can walk into any clinic and get good health care and be treated with dignity and respect. That's an option young women didn't have when I was a teenager. Above all else, have faith in yourself and in God that you will make the right decision. Take a chance on life. Do what you really want to do.

Teen Mothers Must Take Responsibility

. . . We are lucky today that many of the circumstances which made Mosella's experience difficult have changed. It was not legally possible for a single person to use prescriptive contraceptives such as the pill until 1972. Women did not have access to a safe, legal abortion until 1973. That wasn't all that long ago. In addition, it hasn't been socially acceptable to be a single parent until recent years.

Women have reproductive freedom today which years ago they didn't have. This freedom provides more options for a young woman, but it also carries with it responsibility. A young woman must decide for herself how she wants to resolve her pregnancy. Having more options doesn't necessarily make a decision easier; it means there are more decisions to make. In previous years it was socially unacceptable for a young, single woman to raise her baby alone. Today societal views toward teen pregnancy and parenting have changed. Although not everyone shares the same views, teen pregnancy and parenting does not carry the same level of shame it once did. There are some who still see it as a strictly moral issue, that teens should never participate in premarital sex, and these people may judge you for the choices you make. There are others who view parenting as a strictly economical issue. They resent and even protest against their tax dollars being spent to support unwed teens and their children. There are still others who have liberal views. They support and advocate programs to ensure that pregnant teens and their babies are adequately cared for. There is societal agreement about one thing, however, and that is responsibility. No matter which option a teen chooses, whether it is parenting, abortion, or adoption, society expects that she will be responsible. If she chooses to be a parent, it is expected that she will find the resources to support herself and her baby, and that she will continue with her education.

It is also acceptable for a young woman to choose not to be a parent. She can terminate her pregnancy or place her baby for adoption so that she can delay parenting until she is older, has had more life experiences, and feels ready to be a mother. Delaying parenting has its advantages. It gives a young woman the freedom while she is still young to learn more about herself, and to pursue other life goals without the burden of a child. Whereas in previous years young women tended to marry and have their babies at an earlier age, more young women today are living their lives differently. More young women are postponing childbearing until their mid-twenties or later so that they can have the freedom to get more education, travel, or gather other life experiences.

In the 1985 novel *In Country*, by Bobbie Ann Mason, Sam, a young woman, comments about the plight of her pregnant teen friend and says, "It used to be that getting pregnant when you weren't married ruined your life because of the disgrace; now it just ruined your life and nobody cared enough for it to be a disgrace." [A young woman named Sara] echoes a similar thought when she first finds out that she's pregnant. "How could I have let this happen? . . . What am I supposed to do now? My life is ruined." These young women are not alone in the way they think. Unfortunately, too many young women think that their lives are ruined because they are pregnant, and they give up their hopes and dreams. They think they won't be able to accomplish what they want to do. Your life is not ruined, it is not over. Today there are counseling services in place that are nonjudgmental which will help you explore all your options and help you select the one that's right for you. If you choose to raise your child, there are supportive services in place which will help you stay in school and help you to improve your life and the life of your child. There is no reason to give up hope or your dreams, no matter which option you choose.

The ABCs of Unplanned Pregnancy Decisions

Planned Parenthood Federation of America

Planned Parenthood Federation of America is a national organization dedicated to ensuring the right of individuals to make their own reproductive decisions. In the following selection, Planned Parenthood provides a brief primer on the pros and cons of the three options available to teens who are faced with an unplanned pregnancy: parenting, adoption, and abortion. Furthermore, the authors explain, a pregnant teen who chooses adoption has two options: a closed adoption in which her identity and that of the adoptive parents are not disclosed, or an open adoption in which the teen may select the adoptive parents and maintain contact with them and the child. In addition, the authors point out, in some locales a new mother can arrange to put her infant in temporary foster care so she can have more time to decide whether or not to raise her child or place the baby for adoption.

Adult and teenage women often face difficult decisions when pregnancy is unplanned.

- How soon do I have to decide?
- What about raising a child?
- What about placing the baby for adoption?
- What about abortion?

Women may ask this question at many times in their lives—especially when their periods are late. . . .

You have three choices if you are pregnant.

- You can choose to have a baby and raise the child.
- You can choose to have a baby and place your child for adoption.
- You can choose to end the pregnancy.

There is no right or wrong choice for everyone. Only you can decide which choice is right for you. . . .

Raising a Child with a Partner

One of your choices is to continue your pregnancy and raise a child. Being a parent is exciting, rewarding, and demanding. It can help you grow, understand yourself better, and enhance your life.

There are two ways to raise a child.

- You might want to raise the child with a partner.
- You might want to raise the child without a partner.

Most of us look forward to finding a life partner—someone with whom we can share the pleasures, responsibilities, and difficulties of family life. You may want to consider marriage if you intend to parent with a partner.

Marriage is a serious legal contract binding both partners. Each one accepts legal as well as moral and emotional obligations to the other. Every state has its own laws about marriage. If you are under 18, contact your local marriage license bureau or consult your religious adviser to find out about the laws in your state.

Consider premarital counseling if marriage is one of your choices. Taking the time to talk about marriage with a counselor can make a big difference. See a private counselor or get counseling through your church, temple, mosque, or some other community service. Family counseling is also beneficial for all couples, married or not—whenever they consider beginning or expanding a family.

With or without marriage, a life partnership can succeed if both people:

- are deeply committed to make it work
- understand what each expects from the relationship.

Remember: A child can bring joy and many other rewards to a relationship. A child can also strain the best relationship. If your commitment is not solid, the relationship may fail. . . .

Raising a Child Without a Partner

The challenge of raising a child alone can also be exciting and rewarding. It is easier if you find and use all the support you can. Be sure to let family and friends know that you hope for their support before you decide to become a single parent.

Even with the help of your family and friends, being a single parent is not easy. It is often complicated and frustrating. Your child's needs will constantly change and so will your ability to meet those needs. You may want to consider counseling to help you through these changes. You may find out about counseling from your local department of children's services.

Your child will look to you for love and care—all day, every day. And you can take great pleasure helping your child grow into a happy, independent, and responsible adult. But there will be no breaks. It takes years for children to become responsible for themselves. And convenient, affordable childcare is difficult to find.

It takes a lot of money to raise a child. Earning a living for you and your child will be a real challenge—even if you have finished school and can get a good job. Your own parent(s) may find it hard to help you out with all the bills. Welfare payments barely cover the basics.

Because your child will need you so much, you may become more dependent on your own family and friends—for help with the child, for money, and for emotional support. You may have to give up a lot of freedom to be a good single parent. On the other hand, because you will not have to make compromises with a partner, you can raise the child as you wish—with your values, principles, and beliefs.

Parenting requires lots of love and unlimited energy and patience. There will be times when you may feel that you are not doing a good job at it. To feel good about being a single parent, it must be what you want to do—for a long time. You already know what that means if you have other children. If you don't, talk with a single mother or with a counselor who works with single mothers. . . .

Placing the Baby for Adoption

One of your choices is to complete your pregnancy and let someone else raise your child. Many women who make this choice are happy knowing that their children are loved and living in good homes. But some women find that the pain of being separated from their children is deeper and longer lasting than they expected.

There are two kinds of adoption:

- Closed adoption—the names of the birth mother and the adoptive parents are kept secret from one another.
- Open adoption—the birth mother may select the adoptive parents for her child. She and the adoptive parents may choose to get to know one another. They may also choose to have an ongoing relationship.

Adoption is legal and binding whether it is open or closed. Few adoptions are reversed by the courts. You will have to sign "relinquishment papers" some time after your baby is born. After signing, you may be given a limited period of time during which you may change your mind. In most states, minors do not need a parent's consent to choose adoption. However, the child's father can demand custody of the child unless he has already signed release papers for the adoption.

Adoption laws are different in every state. Find out in advance what they are in your state. Talk with an adoption counselor or lawyer before deciding on any arrangement. Be sure to read everything *very* carefully before you sign. It is always best to have a lawyer review all documents first.

There are thousands of women and men waiting to adopt newborn children. However, there is no guarantee that homes will be found for all children waiting to be adopted. This is especially true of children of color and children with disabilities.

Arranging the Adoption

Adoption is arranged in three ways:

- Agency (licensed) adoption: the birth parents "relinquish" their child to the agency. The agency places the child into the adoptive home.
- Independent (unlicensed) adoption: the birth parents relinquish their child directly into the adoptive home.
- Adoption by relatives: the court grants legal adoption to relatives.

All adoptions must be approved by a judge in a family or surrogate court.

You could place your child through a public or private agency that is licensed by the government. These agencies:

- provide counseling
- handle legal matters
- make hospital arrangements for your child's birth
- select a home for your child
- refer you to agencies that may help you financially

Sometimes an agency is able to help find a home for you during your pregnancy. In agency adoption, your name and the adoptive parents' names are usually kept secret. However, some licensed agencies also offer various open adoption options. . . .

You can arrange an independent adoption through a doctor or lawyer or someone else who knows a couple that wants to adopt. Some states have private, independent adoption centers that provide counseling. These centers are run by women and men who want to adopt. Independent adoptions are not legal in some states because there is a risk that birth mothers and adoptive parents may be exploited.

An independent adoption is usually an open adoption. The adoptive parents will often agree to pay for your hospital and medical bills until the child is born. They may even pay for your living expenses during that time. Usually the adoptive parents hire one lawyer to represent them and you. If you choose independent adoption, you should consider having a lawyer of your own. . . .

You will be asked to sign a "take into care" form after you give birth. This allows the adoptive parents to take the child home while the state studies their family life and home environment. The study takes six to eight weeks. During this time, both you and the prospective parents can change your minds. When the study is over, you will be asked to sign "relinquishment papers.". . .

You may want your child to stay in your own family. However, independent adoptions with a relative must also be approved by a family- or surrogate-court judge. Your relatives will have to be studied by a state agency before the adoption can be finalized. And you will have no more right to the child than if you placed it with strangers. . . .

In some cities and counties, temporary foster care may be available for the children of mothers who need more time to decide between adoption and parenting.

You and the child's father must both sign a legal foster care agreement to have another family care for your child. It's a good idea to consider a legal contract even if someone in your family provides the foster care. Legal contracts can help prevent misunderstandings.

Foster care agreements include:
- how often you agree to visit your child
- how long your child will stay with the foster care family
- how much money you may have to pay for the child's care
- how often you must see the social worker

You could lose your child if you don't keep your part of the agreement. It is important to remember that foster care is only temporary and is not a good substitute for a permanent home. . . .

Choosing Not to Continue the Pregnancy

One of your choices is abortion. Abortion is a legal and safe procedure. More than 90 percent of abortions occur during the first 12 weeks of pregnancy.

Vacuum aspiration is the usual method of early abortion. First, the cervix is numbed. Then the embryo or fetus is removed through a narrow tube with vacuum suction. The surgery takes about five minutes.

Early medical abortion is available in a small number of clinics that are participating in clinical trials. This method uses the medication mifepristone or methotrexate. Medical abortion is not yet widely available.

Early abortion is usually done in a clinic, doctor's office, or hospital. You don't need to stay overnight. Most likely, you can return to your normal activities the next day. Abortions performed later in pregnancy may be more complicated but are still safer than having a baby.

Abortion is one of the safest operations available. Serious complications are rare. But the risk of complications increases the longer a pregnancy continues.

Most women say that early abortion feels like menstrual cramps. Other women say it feels very uncomfortable. Still others feel very little.

You will need to sign a form that says you:
- have been informed about all your options
- have been counseled about the procedure, its risks, and how to care for yourself afterward
- have chosen abortion of your own free will

Most teenagers consult their parents before an abortion. But telling a parent is not required in all states. Many states do require a woman under 18 to tell a parent or get a parent's permission. If she cannot talk with her parents, or chooses not to, she can speak with a judge. The judge will decide whether she is mature enough to make her own decision about abortion. If she is not mature enough, the judge will decide if abortion is in her best interest. . . .

Most women feel relieved after an abortion. Some experience anger, regret, guilt, or sadness for a short time. These feelings may be complicated by the abrupt hormonal changes that take place after abortion. Serious, long-term emotional problems after abortion are rare. They are more likely after childbirth.

You are more likely to experience serious regrets after abortion if you have strong religious feelings against it. Be sure to examine your moral concerns before choosing abortion. Counseling is available before and after abortion.

Uncomplicated abortion should not affect future pregnancies.

DIFFERENT REASONS FOR THE SAME CHOICES

Linda Roggow and Carolyn Owens

Linda Roggow, a licensed social worker, is supervisor of social services at New Horizons Adoption Agency in Minnesota. Carolyn Owens is an author and library clerk. The following piece is excerpted from their book *Pregnant and Single: Help for the Tough Choices*. Roggow and Owens provide insights on how some teen mothers decide between parenting, marriage, and adoption. According to Roggow and Owens, pregnant teens should carefully examine their motivations before making a decision about their future and that of their babies. Using case studies of different teens as examples, the authors identify various reasons that teens have given for keeping their child, such as fulfillment of a desire to be needed. In the authors' view, marriage should be an option only if both parents are committed to making the relationship work. Adoption, they note, is another choice made for a variety of reasons, including the conclusion that there is no other alternative.

Being pregnant and single affects women from all areas of society, all economic levels, and all nationalities. Every woman who is pregnant and single lives her own real-life drama of mental, physical, and emotional strain. Each one faces the same choices. . . .

Some of you will choose to live at home, but for others, that will not be an option. Your parents might feel you can't stay there while you're pregnant, or you may not be comfortable living with them.

You may decide to stay with a relative. Perhaps you will need to find other living arrangements. . . .

If you are still in school, you may wonder whether you have to quit. In most schools, you may continue as long as your doctor approves. . . .

There are also schools just for pregnant young women. In some states they are called continuing education or family education centers, and they differ from regular high school. The curriculum includes practical, realistic options for pregnant students. These

Excerpted from Linda Roggow and Carolyn Owens, *Pregnant and Single: Help for the Tough Choices*. Reprinted with permission from Herald Press.

schools give instruction in—
- academic courses.
- prenatal and postnatal care.
- family relations.
- homemaking.
- money and time management.
- career development and personal guidance.

Such centers offer opportunity for peer interaction. The program may last about sixteen weeks, with classes held Monday through Friday, six hours a day. At many of the centers, expectant fathers and future grandparents may also be involved.

Some areas provide a mentoring program that matches teen mothers with successful women in business. The mentors regularly relate with the students and share encouragement, advice, and help. . . .

As a pregnant single, you will want to look at all the options available to you and your child. . . .

Deciding to Keep and Raise a Child

If you have an older sister or girlfriend who's had a baby, you can remember the fascination and excitement of seeing the newborn for the first time. Before the baby was born, perhaps you went to the baby shower and took note of all the darling, tiny outfits. You saw the warm, happy glow on the expectant mother's face. All eyes were focused on her; she was in the "spotlight."

These are all pleasant and wonderful things, but they last only a short time. The spotlight soon dims. Then it's time to take the baby home from the hospital. There are many joys in being a mother. Yet the responsibility of caring for a new life is awesome. Many heartaches and headaches go with the title "Mom.". . .

Unwed mothers have various reasons for deciding to keep and raise their children. . . .

Kelly, aged seventeen, expected her child to fulfill her own desperate need to be loved. "When I was thirteen, my father left us. Mom had to hold down two jobs to support my two sisters and me. She didn't have much time left over for affection."

This was Kelly's second pregnancy After she placed her first baby for adoption, she suffered from a sense of loss and loneliness.

"When I got pregnant this time, I thought now I'd have someone to really love and someone who will love me. I believed I was ready to have another one, settle down, and make a good home. I felt the baby could give me just what I needed.

"The first six weeks with my son were okay. My mom would come over, and all my friends wanted to see the baby and hold him. The newness of it all was exciting! For the first time, I found a purpose in life and really thought someone needed me. All my life I just wanted to be needed."

Kelly's son is now two years old. "I do love him, but I'm finding out it's more than a give-and-take situation. I'm giving, giving, giving, and he's taking, taking, taking. Sometimes I feel drained, with no energy left and little love to give. . . .

"I recognize that my child's needs are important. But it's hard to be loving and to give of myself when I got so little attention in my younger years. There's so much I need for *me*. I know he needs discipline, activities to keep him busy, and loving attention. But it is an endless effort, and I have nothing left for myself."

Kelly looked reflective. "It's real nice when he's sitting in my lap. We cuddle together and rock in the chair. But sometimes he grabs my lipstick when I'm not looking and smears it on the wall. Then it's not so nice."

I Can Be a Good Parent

Carol is a mature nineteen-year-old who was brought up in a positive, loving family environment. "My reason for keeping the baby is that I felt I could parent her responsibly. I wanted to be the one to help my child develop physically, emotionally, and spiritually. I also wanted to work hard toward her overall well-being."

She is realistic and recognizes that there will be ups as well as downs with the responsibility of motherhood. Carol is emotionally mature enough not to depend on the child to make her life happy.

"My own needs are being met through a great family support system. My baby's father is no longer involved, but I have a strong faith in God and can rely on God rather than on myself," she said. "I am highly motivated to parent. . . ."

Her motive was basically good. She felt she could be a good parent, and she had the self-confidence to carry this out. She knew she could give to her baby and didn't need to receive a lot from her baby. . . .

I Have No Other Option

Ann felt trapped. "He's my child, and no one else is going to raise him. I got myself into this, so now I'll just have to suffer." Her family had told her repeatedly, "You must keep your child. There's no other way!"

The neighbor lady had placed her baby for adoption. When Ann's mother heard this, she was horrified: "How in the world could she just up and give away her little baby!"

She got the message. According to her mother, adoption was not the thing to do. Her cultural background said, "You don't give away your own flesh and blood. It's taboo."

She believed the only option was to keep the baby. Her values suggested she was good if she kept the baby, but bad if she released him. As a result, her goals and ambitions were put on hold.

Before long Ann developed resentment toward the whole situation: "My family is well-off and has promised to provide the finances, but I feel locked in, like this is my lot in life.

"I'm graduating in a couple months and would love to go on to college, to be free and do what I want to do. But that's out for a while. I guess I decided to keep the baby because I never saw any other choice."

I Want to Keep My Baby's Father

Ellen based her decision to keep the child on a sincere hope that the baby would force the baby's father to continue their relationship. "I believed that once Charlie watched me go through childbirth and actually saw the baby, he would realize my love for him and give me what I wanted, a wedding. I counted on the delivery room experience to convince him that we should marry.

"I was stunned when he still wanted me to place the baby for adoption. He said he didn't feel we were financially ready. Charlie didn't want to think about settling down or handling the responsibility. He said we'd get married later. That was hard to take. I felt like telling him he could either take the baby and me now or forget it. His attitude was like a slap in the face. I just couldn't understand how he would want to continue our relationship, yet not include our baby."

Ellen never told Charlie that she'd made a decision. "I know how badly he wanted me to let the baby be adopted. But I thought he wouldn't be able to resist his own son. So I kept quiet and hoped he'd change his mind," Ellen stated. . . .

"Charlie really let me have it! 'Ellen, I've told you over and over from the very beginning! Can't you get it through your head? I will not marry you if you keep that kid!' With that, he stomped out of my hospital room.

"Although he'd made it clear where he stood, I refused to give up hope," Ellen said. "After I took the baby home, I figured when he came to visit me, he'd have to see the baby, too. Then he'd understand that I was being a good mother to his son. . . ."

Marriage May Not Be the Solution

Marriage often seems like the best solution to the problem pregnancy, the easiest way out. . . .

If you are ready to settle down, this alternative can be wonderful for all concerned. However, it takes two committed people to make it work.

Marriage is a commitment to a stable union, a lasting relationship between a woman and a man. As two people become a family, each can experience personal growth, joy, and satisfaction while working things out together. . . .

Theresa shared with a support group of pregnant women. She had always dreamed of beginning her family after she and her husband had some time to "just be together and get to know each other."

"I never really wanted to get married until my late twenties,"

Theresa said. "I wanted to experience and savor life before settling down." She shared dreams of travel to Europe, then of time spent raising her horses, which she had entered in shows for several years.

However, the truth is that she is seventeen and pregnant, and the boy she has dated for the past five months wants to marry her.

Theresa's dreams contrast sharply with her current situation. "After thinking it through, I feel I can sacrifice my 'ideal' and commit myself instead to raising my child," she said. "My dreams of travel and horses will have to wait. What still concerns me, though, is whether I want to work at being Steve's wife for the rest of my life."

Steve doesn't have all the qualities she looks for in a husband. He *is* the father of her child. Still, she wonders if she can give up the hope of marrying her dream man. . . .

"My counselor really helped me see some things I hadn't thought about before. She told me, 'There are three major transitions in the lives of most people. They are changes from
- adolescence to adulthood.
- single life to married life.
- non-parenthood to parenthood.'

"Then my counselor explained, 'Each transition takes time. You need to complete one change before moving on to the next one. If you get pregnant and married while you are in your teens, you are forced to make the transitions all at once.'

"What she said made me realize that marriage to Steve is more than slipping rings on our fingers and calling ourselves man and wife. After the honeymoon, there would be big adjustments to make. And they'd be ones we would have to make together, both of us going through them at exactly the same time. . . .

A generation ago, when a woman became pregnant before marriage, the two were honor bound to say, "I do." A lot of these hastily arranged marriages did not result in living happily ever after. Instead, both people felt trapped. Some couples today feel trapped. . . .

The media are filled with fantasies of roses, orange blossoms, and moonlit nights. Such stories hide the thorns and thunderstorms. The movie producers go to extraordinary lengths to portray love and marriage as something magic and mystical.

People say, "Where love is blind, marriage is a great eye-opener." Some of us have been there, in a less-than-perfect marriage. We recommend that couples open their eyes wide *before* entering marriage. . . .

What *benefits* will marriage provide? Do you really believe that three can live as cheaply as one? You would have companionship and never have to worry about a date. You'd have a father for the child, and a husband to help provide for the three of you.

If the benefits outweigh the obstacles, then marriage could be tailor-made for you. Remember that marriage should solve more problems than it creates.

Maybe you're not 100 percent in agreement with marriage to your baby's father. In that case, your next step is to consider adoption.

Considering Adoption as an Option

If you are eighteen or older, the decision about whether to place your baby for adoption must be made by you and by the legally recognized baby's father, if he is eighteen or older. . . . If you or the father is under eighteen, your parents or his parents must sign the adoption papers.

If you are an adult, no one can force you to release your child against your will, unless there is evidence that you have mistreated your child. You have the first right to parent your child.

This is the legal situation in most states and provinces, but laws for your area may vary. . . .

To make an intelligent decision, look at all the options, including the tough choice of adoption. . . .

At age nineteen, Trudy lived in a sparsely furnished, basement efficiency apartment with her two children. One day she called the Child Protection Agency. Her eighteen-month-old had upset her, and Trudy was afraid she would lose control.

Trudy had many emotional needs herself, such as a big desire to be loved and accepted. Her relationships with men had not been positive. Trudy admitted that most of the reason for her anger and hot temper was because she was always trying to please others, never herself.

She had a host of hostile feelings toward her newborn's father, who was not the father of her toddler. Her call to the Child Protection Agency arose out of deep concern for the welfare—even for the life— of her ten-day-old baby.

"I've made so many mistakes with the first child," Trudy mourned. "I don't want to make the same ones with the second baby." Her toddler was unruly and lacked discipline because Trudy felt weak and had unfulfilled desires of her own. She had been in therapy for several months.

Trudy's friends, family, and caseworker recognized her inability to cope with the first child. They all supported Trudy in her decision to place her second baby for adoption.

My Child Needs Two Parents

Karen was an adopted child herself. At age seventeen, the most important thing to her was that her child should have two parents. Karen was brought up in a nurturing home and appreciated her father and mother. Over the years, they had often reminded Karen of the excitement in their hearts the day they brought her home.

Karen had a nineteen-year-old friend who was an unmarried mother; she kept her own little boy, Scott. Karen saw Scott as a child who had no one with whom to go fishing or play ball. The strain of trying to be both mom and dad, in Karen's opinion, could be exhausting.

She chose to take the focus off herself and place it on her child and the child's welfare. She also did not want the stigma of illegitimacy placed on her baby.

As a mature seventeen-year-old, Karen was thoughtful and always doing kind deeds for others, such as volunteer work at the local hospital. She firmly believed the greatest kindness she could give her child was to release him.

Still, her decision didn't come easily. Some of her peers at school gave her a bad time. "People came up to me in the hall and said, 'Oh, how can you do that to your baby, give it away like it's nothing, when babies are just so cute and everything?'

"I told these kids right out that *cute* had nothing to do with it. If they wanted *cute*, they should buy a pet. Babies are not pets. They're people who need all the love in the world."

Karen concluded, "When I'm a parent, I want a husband and a nice place for my family to live."

Too Young

"At fourteen, I'm too young, and I recognize that there really isn't any choice in my situation," Terri shared. "My parents say I can't keep the baby, and that's the end of it. Of course, they can't force me to adopt my child out, but I still need a roof over my head.

"What am I supposed to do?" Terri wondered. "Get an apartment? Take my baby to a daycare center on my bike? Lie about my age to get a job—with no work experience?"

The concluding factor for Terri was that her parents would be unhappy if she kept the child, and probably they would make Terri miserable, too.

"I couldn't live with that," she said.

After her delivery, Terri will release her baby for adoption. "I dream sometimes about my boyfriend and marrying him. But who is to know if we're going to be right for each other a few years down the road? Besides, I'm only fourteen, way too young to be a wife.". . .

Trisha Tells Her Story

The day after I found out about my pregnancy, I knew I had to tell my mom. Here's the shocker: For some reason, Mom strongly suspected and wasn't all that surprised! Still, it took her a week before we could talk about the problem.

I tried to look at it from her angle. I knew that if our roles were switched, I'd be mad, too. I couldn't tell my dad. Mom told him. He didn't say a word. It was something he didn't want to discuss.

As soon as Mom knew, she asked me to talk with our pastor. He strongly urged that I find some counseling, and he advised me to take my time in making any decisions. . . .

When I pictured myself placing the baby for adoption, it was tough. I knew I wouldn't be able to see him or know where he lived. I wouldn't have the chance to see his first tooth or be with him for his first haircut.

One thing that helped was that no one pushed me to make my decision. Right from the beginning, I knew there was a lot of time to make that choice. But that worked against me, because I kept putting it off.

The way I finally made my choice for adoption was to think about the pros and cons. If I kept the baby, then I'd need to quit both school and my job, because Mom worked full-time. I wouldn't have money to live elsewhere, and I would likely end up on Aid for Dependent Children (AFDC). When I wrote the pros and cons on a piece of paper, it was obvious what I should do.

A few people voiced negative reactions. One question came up most often: "How could you give away your baby?" They tried to make me feel guilty, like I was copping out. But when people asked me, I just explained that I couldn't afford to raise a child, that I'm not the only one responsible for him, and that I felt a one-parent home wouldn't be fair to the baby.

After a while, kids at school said they respected me for my decision. The funny thing, though, was that they didn't come right out and tell me. I had to hear it through the grapevine. I wish they'd have come to me and offered some support.

However, my teachers told me face-to-face that they thought I did the right thing. Of course, my parents were relieved. They wanted me to place the baby for adoption and felt it was best all along.

This experience has matured me. I can make decisions better because now I look at all the angles and then decide. My parents and I have grown closer. We communicate more and talk openly about things now. They support me with love.

DECIDING ABOUT ADOPTION

Jeanne Warren Lindsay

Jeanne Warren Lindsay has authored more than a dozen books on adolescent pregnancy and parenting. She also developed and coordinated the Teen Parent Program at Tracy High School in Los Cerritos, California. In the following selection, Lindsay discusses the option of adoption. According to the author, pregnant teens generally do not consider adoption because deciding to part with their child is too painful. However, adoption no longer means that a mother will never see her baby again, Lindsay explains; in fact, many pregnant teens choose open adoption, which enables them to meet the adoptive parents and stay in contact with their child. Lindsay cautions teens to be objective about the advice they receive from others about adoption and to base their decisions on what they think will be best for their baby. She suggests a variety of ways for pregnant teens to learn more about adoption, including talking with birth mothers or people who were themselves adopted as infants.

I was about 14 when I found I was pregnant. The scariest part was telling my mom. I was growing up in one of those families that if you ever get pregnant, you pack your bags and go. I knew I was pregnant because I hadn't had a period.

I waited until 3 A.M., I packed my clothes, cleaned out my dresser drawers, and put my bags by the front door. I woke my mom up and said, "I'm pregnant."

She was sleeping, and she sat up and said "What?" And I jumped off the bed.

"What are you going to do?" she asked.

I started crying and said, "I don't know."

*I told her I thought my only option was abortion. I made an appoint-
ment and she was to go with me, but that morning she told me she
really didn't want me to do that. She said there were other options.*

*The agency we called first said they would not accept interracial
babies, so we went down to Marywood and did the entrance interview. I wasn't sure adoption was what I wanted to do. I went back
and forth between deciding whether to keep the baby or place the
baby throughout the whole pregnancy. One day, "I'm going to
keep," the next day, "I'm going to place." The more I learned about
adoption, the less afraid of it I became.*

Tatum

*I was 14 when I got pregnant. I wasn't expecting it because we
used birth control, but the condom broke. I figured right away that
I was pregnant.*

*I didn't have to tell my parents. My dad knew, and my mom found
out from one of her friends. She was mad at me, and she wanted
me to have an abortion.*

*My boyfriend and I weren't ever really together. He told me he didn't
want to have anything to do with the baby. We talked while I was
pregnant, but we weren't together. He said he would pay for an abortion, but I didn't want that. "What are you going to do?" he asked.*

*I told him I was considering adoption. He never really decided any-
thing. He just went along with whatever I decided.*

Carmen

Few Teens Plan for Adoption

A couple of generations ago, many pregnant teenagers relinquished
(gave up, released, surrendered) their babies for adoption. An unmarried adolescent who became pregnant was often hustled off to Aunt
Agatha's home in Missouri where she lived until her baby was born.
Usually the young mother didn't see her baby at all. It was placed for
adoption with a family she would never meet, and the entire event
was wrapped in secrecy. Her friends were told she was vacationing
with Aunt Agatha, and she was urged to forget the whole episode and
return to "normal" life as a teen.

This picture changed twenty or thirty years ago. Women of all
ages in the United States have a legal right to an abortion during the
early months of pregnancy (although in some states, women younger
than 18 must have either their parent's permission or the court's

approval). Each year about one-third of the million teenage pregnancies end in induced abortion. Another one out of six ends in
spontaneous miscarriage.

Very few teens make adoption plans for their babies, less than four
percent of the half-million who give birth each year in the United
States. There are several reasons that so few pregnant adolescents consider adoption.

First and most important, they, like all pregnant women, bond
with their babies before birth. They love their babies just as older
mothers do, and adoption is an extremely hard and painful decision
to make.

Second, the younger an adolescent is, the less likely she is to make
an adoption plan. Developmentally, people in early adolescence find it
difficult to look ahead. Getting through the pregnancy may be all she
can handle. Trying to figure out what's best for her child and herself for
the next 18 years may be almost impossible. Making any kind of plan
may require more maturity than she has had a chance to develop. . . .

Many pregnant teens do not know how much adoption has
changed in the past decade. If you think that adoption means giving
your baby away to strangers, and you assume you would never see
your child again, adoption may seem impossible.

Teens who are more interested in the adoption option are likely to
be those who plan an open adoption. They choose the adoptive parents for their child, and they plan to stay in contact with their child.

Pregnant Teens Get Lots of Advice

If you're a teenager and you're pregnant, you're probably getting lots
of advice. Some people feel teens are not mature enough to make big
decisions about a baby.

You'll undoubtedly hear, "What do you mean, you'll *keep* that
baby? You aren't old enough to be a parent." These people assume
that "of course" you'll make an adoption plan.

Probably an adoption plan has *not* been made by a number of
young women and their partners because of comments like this.
"We'll show them" is sometimes the reaction—along with the feeling
that, *at the time,* keeping your baby to rear yourself may be an easier
decision to make.

On the other hand, you're probably surrounded by people who
can't believe you'd "give your baby away." Your peers who aren't
pregnant and who don't have children may remind you that your
baby "will be so cute." They may assure you that they'll help with
babysitting. "Of course you can manage," they may say.

Some families are convinced that the only responsible answer to
too-early pregnancy is adoption. A couple of generations ago, most
families felt this way if the young couple was not married. Your family
may remind you of the importance of a child having two parents who

are married and who live together, parents who can financially support themselves and their child. Your child "should" be with another family who can offer these things, they may say.

Or, and this is the more likely scenario, your family may be appalled at the idea of another family rearing your child. "Not our flesh and blood" is a typical remark.

Advice Can Make Decisions Harder

If a woman is past 20 and living on her own, other people's opinions may add stress to her decision-making efforts. However, she, along with her partner, can usually make her own decision. But if you're a teenager, you may wonder how you'll *ever* make a decision that will please everybody.

The answer, of course, is that you probably can't please everybody. Your biggest concern is your baby. Your next biggest concern needs to be yourself. Somehow, you have to figure out the best plan for you and your baby, then help your friends, and especially your family, understand. You need their support.

Too much advice can make decision-making very hard. . . .

> The decision-making process was difficult. Nick came to me and said, "I'm not ready to be a father. I think we should look at adoption."
>
> I was livid. "How can you say that?" I didn't want to be responsible for any information on adoption because then I'd have to think about it.
>
> I was seven months along when, as I was driving home from church, I started crying. I knew I couldn't keep her. It was a fantasy that I could have this baby and the world be the way I wanted it to be. I went home and told my mom, and we both sat at the kitchen table crying.
>
> Kathleen

As with the less important decisions you make each day, the more you use good judgment and clear-headed thinking to work out your final adoption or parenting plan, the more your family will concur. . . .

Making the Decision

If most pregnant teenagers *choose* to keep their babies to rear themselves, their decision must be respected. It is possible for a young single mother to do a fine job of parenting, especially if she has a good support system within her family. But is that choice consciously made? Or is becoming a mother often simply acceptance of what seems to be—that if one is pregnant and doesn't get an abortion, one will usually have a baby (true), and therefore raise that baby oneself (not necessarily true)?

Many young women are "successful" mothers. They give their children the care they need, sometimes at great sacrifice to themselves. They love their children deeply. But it is difficult to know who will be a good parent and who will not, whether that parent is single or married, 15 or 25 years old. Some 25-year-old parents neglect their children. And sometimes a 15-year-old does a beautiful job of mothering.

Nita and Joe: A Case Study

Nita, 15, and Joe, also 15, were shocked at their positive pregnancy test. They figured they would keep their child, but soon after they took Zach home from the hospital they realized they were not ready to parent. Nita explained:

> Joe was in denial for a couple of months. I figured I'd have my baby, I'd raise it, and then I'd have my life. But it didn't work out that way.

> After Zach was born, I didn't want to hold him. I loved him, but I didn't have that motherly instinct. I was concerned for him, but I really wanted to be a teenager.

> I moved in with Joe and his mother so I could go to a school with childcare. Zach and I went back and forth to school on the city bus, but he kept getting sick.

> My grandma had always talked to me about adoption. Then I was talking to a counselor at school about my problems, and she said it wasn't too late for adoption. Zach was two months old then. I mentioned it to Joe, and he said he'd been thinking about it, too, but he didn't say anything because he didn't want to upset me.

> We decided to go ahead. We talked to an adoption counselor, and we picked out a couple. Three weeks later Zach was gone.

> I didn't have regrets but I was very disappointed in myself. I've been through so much in my life, and I always wanted my child to have a mother and father who would always be there, and who wouldn't ever have money problems.

> My mom had me when she was 17, and she's right now still trying to get back her wild years.

> My mother was very, very sad about the adoption, and she had to go to counseling. My brother and sister took it hard. I'm trying to teach my sister that having a baby may look like fun. It looks easy, but it isn't.

Teens tend to think "My baby will love me. I'll dress him up all cute and everybody will love me." But they aren't looking at the late nights, the crying. They aren't thinking, "How am I going to get to the doctor when I can't even drive yet?" I didn't like relying on other people.

Joe commented:

When I finally realized I would be a father, I was all happy. Nita mentioned adoption back then, but I said, "Let's keep it. We can handle it." So I quit going to school, and I got a job.

It didn't work out. We couldn't afford him, and we weren't even living together after she went back home. She and my mom didn't get along.

I started thinking about adoption after Zach was born. He was more expensive than I thought—the diapers, the formula . . . and sometimes I'd miss out on work because I had to watch him.

We were all sad. When I'm in my room by myself, I think about him. It's getting better as time goes by. We're getting pictures of the baby pretty often.

I want to parent when I can afford it, when I have a place of my own—maybe when I'm 30!

"Nobody Knew"

Often a young woman keeps her pregnancy secret from everyone for several months:

Nobody knew for several months except the birth father. I was 16, and I didn't want to accept reality. Then when I finally accepted it, I didn't want to let anybody know because I had let people down.

The birth father would call and ask what he could do, but I kind of pushed him out, too. I wanted to do this on my own, and I see now that wasn't a good thing.

Finally I let my closest aunt know. She said, "Are you sure?"

I said, "Yes. I sit in class and feel the baby moving. So she came over and told my parents. That was very emotional, the first time I ever saw my father cry.

We found an agency we liked, and that was the best thing that happened. I enrolled there the last 1 1/2 months, and they helped me a lot with information and sorting out my thoughts on what I would do.

During all this time I was alone, I thought, "I'm not ready for this. I don't want my child to come into this world and not have what I have."

I wanted her to have two parents, and I wanted her to have more than I could give. I didn't have a job, and I didn't want to rob her of anything. So I decided adoption was best.

Yvette

If you, like Yvette, are not talking to anyone about your pregnancy, that may be the first thing you need to do. . . . Your family may be more supportive than you expect.

Parents Can Help

Sonia, like so many teens, had a hard time telling her parents she was pregnant. When she finally did, their support became an important part of her decision-making:

I was 16, a junior in high school, and Jake and I had been together about six months. I knew I was pregnant that first month. I went into denial—I didn't tell anybody, not even Jake. I was on the track team, running five miles a day cross-country.

I knew my being pregnant would hurt my parents, and I didn't know how to approach them. I was scared, and I withdrew from them and from all my friends. I didn't want to be around anybody. I wore baggy clothes. The first time I felt him move inside me I just wanted to die.

When I finally told Jake I was pregnant, he was as scared as I was.

Then one day I woke up and realized this baby was important. Somehow I knew it was not for me, but I needed to take care of it. I told my parents, and they were real upset. I had never seen my dad cry before. My brothers were very upset, too.

After a few days they came around with "We're going to support you in whatever you decide to do." That meant the world to me. I don't think I could have gone through it without my mom.

Placing Joshua was the hardest thing I ever did in my life. It changed my life, turned my life around and made me a better person. If I had it to do over again, I would place him again, even with what I went through with Jake. I live with it every day of my life. Not a day goes by that I don't think of Joshua. His happiness keeps me going.

Talking with a Birthmother Helps

Maggie, pregnant at 17, worked part-time in an office with a birthmother who talked about her child's adoption. Otherwise, Maggie might never have considered an adoption plan:

Six years ago I got pregnant, three months before I graduated.

I didn't know anything about adoption—it's not talked about much. But I was lucky to be working with a girl who had gone through an adoption, and I knew about it because she was very open.

If it had not been for her, I might never have thought about adoption.

If you don't know much about adoption, one of the best things you can do is find a birthparent, either an individual or a birthparent support group, and learn about their experiences. Maggie continued:

I always thought I would go to college, get married, then have kids, in that order. And I knew I wasn't emotionally ready to parent.

So after this friend and I talked, I called a counselor at an agency. She explained all about adoption and all the different ways to go about it. That's what I liked, the flexibility where you and the adoptive parents make the decisions.

The father was out of the picture because we had broken up. I did tell him, and at first he was supportive. Then a few days later he came over and told me he didn't want to have any more to do with me, no matter what I wanted to do.

I felt I couldn't give my child either the emotional or financial support I had growing up. This was important to me. I was scared, especially as to what people would think of me. I was afraid people would think I was uncaring, and didn't love my child. But I knew that wasn't so.

I tried not to become attached to my baby while I was pregnant, but of course you do.

I had a good support system with my friends and my mother. It was hard to do, and I can't imagine going through it without support.

Do you know adopted children who have known they were adopted, that they are "special," for as long as they can remember?

For some birthparents, hearing from adoptees how they feel about adoption helps:

> *They had a program at the maternity home where you could meet people who had adopted. They brought their children to a picnic, and I said I'd babysit. There was a little girl who was three, another seven or eight, and another who was ten, and all three were adopted. They knew much more about adoption than I did.*
>
> *The youngest little girl asked me, "Are you going to have your baby adopted?"*
>
> *I said "What do you know about adoption?"*
>
> *She said, "I'm adopted and I have two sets of parents. My mommy says I'm more loved because I have four parents." Then she said, "Your baby would be so loved"—this from a three-year-old!*
>
> *I also got to meet my counselor's two adopted children, a daughter two years older than me, and a son four years older. I told her they were so like her and she said, "You know they are adopted???" And I was thunderstruck because they seemed so happy.*
>
> *I started thinking more and more about adoption.*

Tatum

Having, caring for, and loving children are joyful situations for many people. It is an especially joyful happening if the timing is "right." Parenthood at 17—or even 15—may be right for some people. But postponing parenthood for a few years might make it more joyful for others.

Adoption is an option!

DECIDING WHETHER TO GO BACK TO SCHOOL

Danny Gong

In the following selection, Danny Gong examines the reasons why most teen mothers do not return to school even when they realize that they will probably not be able to find a good job without a diploma. While some teen mothers did not like school before they became pregnant, Gong explains, most want to return but are unable to because they cannot find acceptable day care for their children. According to Gong, this situation makes it especially difficult for teen mothers who are on welfare because they risk losing their benefits if they do not return to school. To increase the likelihood that teen mothers will decide to complete their education, he asserts, schools and communities must provide more day care facilities, night schools, and weekend classes. At the time that this article was originally published, Gong was a high school student and a reporter for *New Youth Connections,* an independent newspaper written by and for young people in New York City.

After her only son, Sequan, was born, on March 6, 1995, Linda Vargas knew she wanted to go back to 11th grade. She also knew it wasn't going to be easy.

She couldn't afford to bring her baby to a nursery, and the father gave her practically nothing for their child.

She also didn't want to go on welfare.

"I hated going to the welfare office. It was disgusting, and I did not want to seem like a bum," she said.

But in the end, Linda decided that going on welfare was the only way for her to return to school.

She found an alternative high school where she could make her own schedule and where she receives lots of support from her teachers. . . .

There are an estimated 10,000 to 14,000 teen moms in New York City, and, like Linda, many of them know that balancing school and a baby can be really tough.

Excerpted from Danny Gong, "Books and Babies: A Balancing Act," *New Youth Connections*, May/June 1998. Copyright ©1998 Youth Communication/New York Center, Inc. Reprinted with permission.

It can be so tough, in fact, that less than one-third of teens who have kids before age 18 complete high school, according to the National Campaign to Prevent Teen Pregnancy.

Unlike Linda, many teen moms don't go back to school even after they are on welfare, so they don't get enough of an education to support themselves and their kids later in life.

But new laws that were passed by Congress in 1997 are forcing teen moms on welfare to return to school, or enroll in a GED class or job-training program. Otherwise, they will lose their welfare benefits.

And it's important for all teen moms to go back to school because under the new laws, no one can receive welfare for more than five years, no matter what.

So moms are going to have to learn to support themselves one way or another.

If they don't, and if they really do enforce these laws, in five years they will have no money, no medical benefits, no education, and they will have a child and themselves to support.

It all sounds pretty scary—and it is—but some teen moms think these new laws could be positive.

"I think that it's great, because [otherwise teen moms] will get used to staying home and doing nothing. And this way they can get an education," Linda said.

Help Is Needed

When Linda first went back to school, she relied on her mother, who worked nights, to help her take care of her son.

But she felt bad about it, and she found school boring. So for several months she dropped out and worked as a cashier.

"I hate the job," she said with an annoyed look. "I did not want to spend the rest of my life behind a register."

Finally, Linda decided it was better to go on welfare—which would pay for Sequan's medical and child care expenses—and be in school, and she returned.

Every day now, Linda cooks, wakes up Sequan, feeds him, dresses him and takes him to the Hudson Guild Center's preschool. Then she goes to her new school, West Side Community HS in New York City.

Linda's glad that she's in school because she thinks that by getting a high school diploma, she can get a better job with a higher paying salary.

"And," she said, "I wanted to show my son what I could do."

But even though these new welfare rules might really motivate some moms, lots of people are concerned that the government is not doing enough to help teen moms deal with the difficulties of returning to school.

The schools need to offer support for teen moms who will be returning to school after long absences, and who might not have liked school that much in the first place.

Otherwise, many of them will just drop out like they did before.

But mainly, teen moms need help finding good day care so they'll know that their kids are safe and well cared for when they're in school. At the moment, there just isn't enough day care to go around.

To do this would require a lot of money, and it might take a lot of time to put these social services into effect. But so far, only small steps have been taken.

"Ultimately, if young people's needs are not taken care of now, they are going to suffer terribly," said Pat Beresford, the senior policy analyst for the New York City Comptroller's Office and the head of a task force on teen pregnancy and prevention. She was once a teen mother herself.

Day Care Is Urgent—and Lacking

The biggest problem right now is day care. Here are some of the facts.

Only 41 high schools out of 201 in New York City have day care centers. Altogether, they hold 700 babies.

These centers (called LYFE centers) can be really great for teen moms and their kids. In the center I visited, there were four toddlers in a room, and each room had a certified sitter.

Pictures of Bert and Ernie were hanging near the windows, and there were toys scattered about on the floor.

At the centers, moms get support from counselors, and their children are so close that they can check on them throughout the day.

Nina Suazo, 20, who gave birth to a daughter, Alexa, at 18, now attends City-As-School, an alternative school, and one of the 41 high schools that have day care.

Nina is supported by her husband so it's easier for her to be in school. Still, Nina dropped out of school for a while, but she felt like she was "wasting time. I wanted to go to school to take care of my daughter and not just depend on my husband."

Having her baby in a LYFE center makes that easier for Nina.

"Knowing that my baby is in good hands gives me relief. I am able to function better in school not having to worry about Alexa so much," said Nina.

But while the city plans to expand these programs, they won't have space for the majority of kids.

That wouldn't be so bad, but it's unclear whether moms will be able to find day care any place else.

Most teen moms will have to go to private day care centers or find a neighbor or family member to watch their kids during the day.

The big problem is that thousands of moms in New York City are already on waiting lists to get their kids into day care centers.

And some private day care centers are refusing anyone on welfare because the city often has been behind in paying for their services.

The city is trying to fix the problem. The mayor's 1998 budget has more than doubled the amount of money to be spent on day care for moms on welfare.

But currently, Ms. Beresford said, "there's just an absolute insufficient supply [of day care]."

I Need a Baby-Sitter . . . Please

And if they can't find day care, many teen moms—even those who want to get an education—will have to remain at home to watch their kids.

When welfare ends after five years, they will find themselves scrambling to find a job without an education. That won't help them, or society.

"If teen moms can prove that they cannot find adequate day care, they don't have to go to school," Ms. Beresford said, "But their clock will continue to tick."

Day care has been a problem for Tawanda, 19, who had a son in the fall of 1997. She had already graduated high school when she had her baby, but she knew she wanted to go on to college.

Tawanda became pregnant during her senior year of high school, and graduated in June 1997 with an 89 average, six months pregnant. But because she couldn't find affordable day care, she has not been able to work or go to college.

"I want to work my butt off, but there's no baby-sitter and the day care centers around here are three hundred and fifty bucks a week," she said, and welfare just doesn't cover that much.

Nearly a year after she graduated, Tawanda finally found a relative to watch her son, who the city will pay $150 every two weeks.

Now she will be able to attend LaGuardia College in the fall of 1998 and will work at the Museum of Natural History in June 1998.

"Having my son has motivated me to go back to college because I want to make more money," she said.

"I hope that my son, Shaliek, will accomplish things. And I hope and pray that he doesn't make the same mistakes that I did," she added.

But if Tawanda hadn't found a family member to look after her son, she might still have been stuck at home.

A Second Chance for Independence?

Although it definitely seems like a fabulous idea for teen moms to be required to go back to school, the lawmakers aren't adequately addressing the many different problems that exist in a big city.

If they do address these problems, teen moms will have a second chance to get an education and to be independent.

Lots of teens think that if they get pregnant, they'll take responsibility and raise their kids right. But after the baby is born, they find out that "taking responsibility" isn't easy, and they wind up going on welfare.

In the long run, requiring a teen mom to finish her education is asking her to be responsible. But teen moms can't do this alone—they do need help.

Now that Nina has returned to school, she plans to go on to college to study medicine.

She quit all of her old ways—like cutting school and hanging out in the streets—because she didn't want to set a bad example for her daughter.

"Alexa comes first," Nina said.

If teen moms get an education, more of them will get good jobs and be off welfare. If that happens for at least some teen moms, then the reforms will have succeeded.

But if we don't help out teen moms, these laws could be a bunch of bureaucratic bull that could really just hurt teen moms and their kids rather than helping. . . .

Going Back to School Is Hard

With thousands of teen moms expected to return to school, teachers, principals and counselors are going to have to face a tough reality: Most teen moms will be returning to the classroom behind in their education, and many may have a pretty hard time catching up.

What's more, many teen moms just don't want to be in school in the first place. In fact, about 50% of teen mothers drop out before getting pregnant.

"Some feel too old and don't want to go to school. Some just don't like school. Some feel bad that they can't keep up," said Vera Thigpen of the Teen Age Services Act Program, who helps teen moms become self-sufficient.

Even for moms who were good students, going back to school can be hard, and they usually need extra help.

When Linda went back to school after being out for just a few months, she decided to go to an alternative school, which made her life easier.

"I choose my hours and classes that fit my schedule. Also, no one knows me and they can't judge me. I consider my teachers as my second parents because they're always there for me. They listen," Linda said.

Linda might have found life a lot more difficult, and she might have been much more uncomfortable, if she had gone back to an ordinary school.

And Linda *wanted* to return to school.

But many teen moms who will be forced back because of welfare reforms won't be so enthusiastic and will probably need a lot more encouragement and support if they're going to succeed.

New Ways to Help Are Needed

Young moms need social services, like a teacher they can talk to or a counselor, said Ms. Beresford. Young moms have a lot of extra worries on their minds.

"It doesn't necessarily have to be someone who is licensed; it could be anybody, just so they can express their feelings," Ms. Beresford said.

But because the Board of Education has very real problems of space and money, and because many teen moms don't want to go back to regular schools, the majority of teen moms go to GED courses, which usually don't have a day care or support services.

"I think the Board of Education will be addressing these problems. It's to their best interest to do so," said Ms. Beresford. But she also said it's a slow process, and that setting up the programs will cost money.

"There's got to be the will to do it," she said.

Schools and GED centers do need to provide more support services. But expanding night schools and offering weekend classes might help even more, said Ms. Beresford.

Because most people work on weekdays, it is much easier for teen moms to find someone, like a friend or relative, to watch their kids at night or on weekends.

Right now there are two night high schools in the city, but some others that used to be open were closed.

Ms. Beresford knows how important night school can be. She gave birth to her first child at 18, and spent the next 10 years attending college at night before she graduated and started a successful career.

Ms. Beresford said it's really important to find ways to help teen moms go back to school now, because if we don't, in the long run, it's more likely that their "kids will be hungry, or they'll put their kids in foster care, or they'll find illegal ways of making money."

In the end, that won't be good for anybody.

CHAPTER 4

IT HAPPENED TO ME: YOUNG MOTHERS SPEAK OUT

WHEN I WAS GARBAGE

Allison Crews

California teen Allison Crews discovered she was pregnant at the age of fifteen. Because she had been taught that teen mothers never finish school and are a burden on society, Crews explains, she initially thought of herself as "garbage" for getting pregnant. She describes how she was pressured to put her baby up for adoption by her family, prospective adoptive parents, and the adoption facilitator the state required her to consult. This pressure served to intensify her lack of confidence and self-worth, Crews writes, and it was not until she gave birth that she gained the emotional strength to insist on keeping her son. Crews asserts that she is not "garbage" but an excellent mother who is continuing her education while raising her son.

When I was in 10th grade, I skipped a week of school. I was too scared, too humiliated, too sick and weak to leave my house. A week away from school earned me two weeks of "in-school suspension." Ten full school days I had to sit in a boxed-in desk, in a 6-by-20-foot room. Yellowing posters of needles and bottles of beer proclaiming "JUST SAY NO!" hung crookedly on the walls. I was allowed to go to the bathroom only twice daily, for 15 minutes. When you are five weeks pregnant, 30 minutes a day is hardly adequate for throwing up.

I sat at my desk, 15 years old, failing in school, pregnant, sick and terrified. I sat at my desk, rubbing my still-flat stomach and clenching my jaw tightly to hold down my vomit. "Two more hours and I can throw up," I reassured myself. I replayed the moment of truth in my mind millions of times during those two weeks. The moment I saw the second line appear on the pregnancy test stick. POSITIVE. POSITIVE. POSITIVE. But from that moment on, I wasn't positive about anything. Except the fact that I needed desperately to vomit. I wrote furiously in my blue velvet–covered journal, tearing the pages with my Hello Kitty pen and smearing the ink with my tears. Fantasies of virgin-white wedding dresses and sponge-painted nurseries unfolded on those blank pages, in the brief moments after bathroom breaks, when my fears were purged and flushed away. Incoherent poems and

Reprinted from Allison Crews, "When I Was Garbage," *Girl-Mom*, www.girlmom.com. Reprinted with permission from the author.

pessimistic single-line entries poured out during the rest of the long days. Many pages read only "NO!" in bold letters, traced over and over, the impressions appearing on the next several pages.

I remembered facts I had learned as a freshman in "sex-education" about teenage pregnancy. Teenage mothers are a burden to society. The children of teenage mothers inevitably become crack-addicted gang members. Teenage mothers never successfully complete high school, let alone attend college. These weren't just statistics, I was led to believe, but invariable truths. I had become garbage, worthy only to sit in my isolated desk and cry to myself and throw up in a dirty bathroom stall. I was a pregnant teenage girl.

Revealing the Secret

After my two weeks of suspension, I forced my pregnancy to hide in the depths of my mind. Thoughts of my future and of becoming a mother all but disappeared, forced to linger with memories of child-hood and homework assignments. It was forgotten. My boyfriend and three friends who knew of my pregnancy assumed I would abort. I was not the type of girl who becomes a mother. Months began to pass, and the only sign of pregnancy were my swollen breasts and an infrequent fluttering in my belly. These signs, undetectable to anyone but myself, dredged up the fears that I thought I had buried so well. I was actually pregnant, I began to realize again, more clearly than I had since those two weeks I had spent in isolation, with only my thoughts and my morning sickness. I continued to hide my pregnancy, even as it became more and more obvious.

School was dismissed during my sixteenth week of pregnancy. My boyfriend and I were engaged in another vicious, mud-slinging fight. He threw the lowest blow. At the time I was so enraged and angry that I could not imagine a more evil act being committed. He told my parents I was pregnant. I realize now what an amazing thing he did for me, although his intent at the time was only to cause me pain. My pregnancy was real. Not only to me, but also to my parents, to my sister, to my relatives, to my newly appointed obstetrician. I was having a baby. There was no turning back. I watched a fuzzy little worm of a baby dance across a television screen, as I lay on a long sheet of wax paper, my stomach exposed and covered in chilled jelly. This was what had been causing me to vomit. This was what had been causing me to outgrow every bra I owned. This was what had caused me so much heartbreak and pain those first few weeks. What appeared to be a hand raised up, next to what appeared to be a head. "Hello mommy!" my 60-something-year-old OB said in a squeaky voice that I assumed was supposed to be a baby's. "I'm a baby boy." I realized then that this little worm that had caused my life to turn upside down in a matter of weeks was no worm at all. He was my son.

It was assumed my son would be given up for adoption, just as a few weeks earlier it had been assumed he would be aborted. I am not sure who made this decision. But it was not me. I wanted to be a good mother. My beautiful, fuzzy black and white son, who swam inside of me like a fish, deserved only the best. No mother under that magical age of 18 could provide that, and, being that I was only 15, I would have to let somebody else raise him. That was the "right" thing to do. My boyfriend and I met with a lovely couple. A very rich, childless couple. While I enjoyed their company at dinner, and definitely enjoyed the food that they bought for me, I did not want them to be the parents of my son. I wanted my boyfriend and I to be his parents. We *were* his parents. The boyfriend and I left dinner that night, walking ahead of the lovely couple and my parents.

"We can call your lawyer and work out the rest of the details this week," my mom cooed to the lovely wife.

"I guess we made our decision," my boyfriend whispered. I was trapped.

"I Want My Baby"

I did call the lawyer, we did work out details. I cried myself to sleep every night for the next four months, staining my navy blue pillowcases. I wanted desperately to be a mother, not simply a baby machine for such a lovely couple. The lovely wife, I learned one night after Lamaze class, was pregnant. Relief flooded my swelling body. "I can keep my baby!" I silently rejoiced. "I have diapers to buy, clothes to wash, car seats to find, nursing bras and slings to sew!"

"We still want to adopt, though. You know our history of miscarriage."

"Oh well. I guess I can't keep my baby after all." I was deflated.

Sure enough, the lovely wife miscarried at 12 weeks. She called me nightly, crying and thanking me for giving her my son. I was, she told me, the only thing that kept her from giving up on life. My son and me. *"Our* baby" became his name while she talked to me on the phone. She gave me weekly reports of how the nursery was coming along (complete with a 2,000 dollar classic Pooh mural, which I am sure would make a world of difference to a newborn), the hundreds of dollars they were spending on clothes, how excited their family was, and how much they loved "our baby" already. The hole got deeper. I couldn't crawl, scratch or shovel my way out. By law in California, birth mothers must meet with an "adoption facilitator." This mediator "counsels" you and explains the process of adoption to you. I repeatedly told her, over the course of two months, "Lisa, I don't want to do this! I want my baby!"

"Well, I want to take a cruise to the Bahamas. But if I took a cruise to the Bahamas, I wouldn't have money left for rent or food. Sometimes what we want isn't what is best."

Oh, yes, babies and cruises are so similar! How could I have been so blind? I later learned that adoption facilitators, while required by the state, are not employed by the state. Prospective adoptive parents employ adoption facilitators. At the time, I wasn't aware of this. I believed this woman. I was selfish to want to raise my son. How could I be so selfish? (She did use the word "selfish.") Pregnant teens are garbage. Once the baby is born, the mother becomes even smellier garbage, dependent on her parents and society's tax dollars to support her children. I had to do something to hoist my son above the metaphorical garbage bin. I had to give him to this lovely couple; they were not garbage, like I was.

An Early Morning Dash to the Hospital

I grew during those weeks, not only physically (60 pounds!) but emotionally and spiritually. I meditated, prayed, screamed, cried, slept, wrote, read and thought. I realized I was more capable than I was being led to believe. I made my decision, 38 weeks into my pregnancy. I informed my boyfriend of this decision. "I am keeping the baby. I don't care what anyone says or feels. I *will not* lose my son. They want any baby, and I only want mine!" My boyfriend and I were going to tell my parents the next evening at dinner. I fell asleep quickly, not sobbing into my pillow like I had grown used to doing during those pain- and growth-filled three months. I was keeping my baby.

I woke up to go to the bathroom that night at around 2 A.M. As I waddled to the bathroom, I looked down the hallway and saw my boyfriend typing away at the computer, talking to some stranger on the internet, like he usually did while staying the night. Then came the gush. "John! My water broke!" I panted, attempting to jog down the hallway. Then came the pain. "John! I am having contractions already! It wasn't like this in the Lamaze videos! The women in those never got contractions so fast—there must be something wrong with me! I gripped the edge of my kitchen counter, and watched the clock on the microwave. Six minutes apart, the orange numbers informed me. I stayed calm, just like I had planned. I packed my bag, brushed my teeth, wrote e-mails to all of my pregnant friends online, wrote in my journal and cried. I forced my mom to drive me to the hospital at 5:15 A.M. She didn't believe I was really in labor, but still told me, "OK, I will call the lovely couple and let them know to start driving down." She said this in the middle of a contraction.

"No! Don't you pick up that #%@!ing phone! This is my baby. Got it?"

She told me we would "talk about it after the baby came."

An Excellent Mother

The baby came at 8:02 A.M., November 20, 1998. My labor was natural, painful, and beautiful. I held my tiny infant son in my shaking arms, tears running off of my face and onto his still-purple hands. He was so much more than I could have dreamed, so much more than a fuzzy little worm ultrasound baby. He spent three days in oxygen as a result of inhaled amniotic fluid. I was terrified of the lovely couple stealing my new son from the nursery, so I woke every hour to walk quickly and quietly down the hall, into the nursery, to see if he was still there.

He was. I checked the machines he was hooked up to, making sure his oxygen saturation levels and heart and breathing rates were what the nurses expected them to be. They were. I would pad down the hallway, back into my room, rubbing my soft, wrinkled tummy and pull out my new breast pump. I pumped and pumped, watched TV, and imagined that it was my tiny baby extracting milk from my breasts. I had an abundance of precious golden milk that only a mother could make. That is what I was.

My father told the lovely couple that I decided to keep my son. The lovely husband cursed at him, cursed my boyfriend, told my father I was a piece of trash and hung up. The lovely wife called a few days after I brought the baby home to say that she did not hate us. She also said that when I "changed my mind and things got too hard," I could always call them to adopt him. We never spoke again.

Cade Mackenzie is now a happy 24-pound, 8-month-old. He sleeps in my bed, and is happiest when he is nursing, watching Teletubbies, or listening to Bob Marley. I am not a burden to society, my son is not a burden on me. I have received the "Teen Mom Look" from anonymous strangers more times than I can count, but have learned not to be offended but to turn the other way and hold my son even tighter to my chest. I am graduating a semester early, and attend a wonderful home-school program, which allows me to spend my days at home, raising my son. And contrary to what fear-based sex education classes, lovely couples and wonderful counselors had led me to believe in the past, contrary to what I had written so many times in my blue velvet–covered journal, I am not garbage. I am a mother. I may not have blown out 18 candles on a birthday cake, but I am an excellent mother.

A Pregnant Teen's Journal

Andrea Hyravy

Andrea Hyravy gave birth to a son when she was fifteen years old. From the time she first thought she might be pregnant, she wrote down her innermost thoughts and feelings in the journal excerpted here. Hyravy candidly describes her fear of being pregnant and her reaction when her pregnancy was confirmed. She writes of the fluctuations in her relationship with her nineteen-year-old boyfriend and of her mixed feelings about their marriage plans. Above all, she frankly chronicles her constantly changing emotions—one day being pregnant is exciting, another day it is unbearable; one day she is almost resentful toward her baby, another she cannot wait to hold him; one day she is confident her boyfriend loves her, another she is not sure if he cares about her at all. Although proud of her son, Hyravy admits that being a parent is harder than she had anticipated, that she misses going out with her friends, and that neither she nor her boyfriend are ready for marriage.

January 21, 1998: Right now my biggest worry is the most dreaded of a teenage girl's life—pregnancy. I have skipped two periods in a row, but I haven't had any other symptoms besides frequent urination. There is *no* way I can tell Mom and Dad! We talked about abortion if I was, but I know Scott would never be able to go through with it. All I can do is pray I'm not pregnant and (if I am) pray for a miscarriage.

Afraid and Alone

February 9: People make me sick. I desperately need to talk to someone about this pregnancy bullshit, someone besides Scott. But no one wants to listen; nobody wants to hear how alone I feel or how scared I am. I am absolutely terrified. I don't want to get a doctor's appointment because I don't want to be told I'm pregnant. I mean, I've had zero symptoms except my last period was in November. And if I'm not pregnant, then what the hell is wrong with me? I'm just assuming I am, in which case I have no idea what to do. How come everyone else can sleep with anyone and everyone and never get pregnant, but

I have sex with someone I love and trust 100% and I probably am? It's not fair. I'm just so very afraid. I'll have to deal with whatever happens when I get there, but I think (hope) I can manage. And if not, it's nothing that can't be fixed. I'm just glad I have Scott's support! . . .

February 19: My God. If there is one thing that is really retarded, it's when your parents buy you a pregnancy test and make you piss in a plastic Dixie cup. Right now they're hovering over the tester, trying to decide if it's a – or a +. What I hated most was having to discuss all this with them. Now I'm freaking out because I'm scared to death of knowing the results. I can't believe they haven't said anything yet. Is that good or bad? I feel like crying; I rarely get this scared about anything, but the silence makes it worse. What if I'm pregnant? Mom refuses to discuss aborting it, but everything will be over with if I have to have it. Why didn't I think of the consequences *before* we were stupid and started being careless? I want to blame Scott, but it's not like he was the only one involved. I just wish they would *say* something. I don't want to ask, because I don't want them to see me cry or know how afraid I am.

OH MY GOD. Why am I pregnant? I called Scott, and he took it pretty well. Now I'm waiting while he tells his mom. I don't know what to think. I'll have to quit school when I start showing. How can I show my face at church? How can I show my face *anywhere*? The sad thing is, Scott is kind of looking forward to it. But I'm convinced it's a neverending nightmare. I don't want to think about baby names, responsibilities, and "custody" arrangements. I don't even want a baby! I'm so scared. Why didn't I think? . . .

February 22: The time since my last entry has been totally crazy. I'm trying to quit smoking, I can hardly stay awake, and I've been pissed off all the time. Plus too many people have found out. I'm afraid to go to school because so many people have asked me about it, and it upsets me. I'll just be glad when everyone knows and they stop gossiping about it. . . .

February 25: I don't understand why people are so cruel. It seems like the entire school knows I'm pregnant, and instead of asking me, they ask other people. I think the whole day has been dedicated to getting the "real" story.

An Emotional Rollercoaster

April 29: I still have mixed feelings about the baby. Generally, I'm excited and happy about being a mother and influencing the life of a child, and I look forward to the change in me and Scott's relationship. But at other times I'm afraid and angry, almost resentful, toward the baby and the idea that my days of teenage fun are over no sooner than they began. Also, I'm not quite sure Scott realizes how much this is going to affect us, financially. . . . I'm also scared we aren't meant to be together. We aren't getting married until I graduate, but by then we will have been together for 4 years. Can we possibly last that long with a child, and as young as we are? What if this isn't the right thing for either of us? . . .

May 17: I finally talked to Scott about all the stuff that's been on my mind. We got in a fight, but things worked themselves out. He reassured me of his feelings for me, which I think was a lot of the problem, and I've promised myself that I'll trust him and stop being so damn paranoid. Just 8–12 more weeks of being pregnant! I cannot express how glad I am. Not just because I won't be fat anymore (hopefully), but because I'm very excited about being a mom and sharing something so meaningful with Scott. It really is a miracle that the two of us created another life, a real human being. Everyone is being really supportive, more so than I thought. . . .

June 16: Week 32—just 4–10 more! Every day I get more excited about my son's birth. I can't wait to hold him and look at him and talk to him and spoil him rotten! It's weird to think that, right now, he is 100% dependent on me. If I died, he would die unless he got prompt medical attention. But he could be born tomorrow and he would be just fine. He's in my belly with hair and fingernails, eyes that can see, ears that can hear; a mouth that tastes, sucks his thumb, and cries! He is almost ready for life outside my body. It's hard to believe I was so negative about this same baby just four months ago. I can't believe we actually talked about abortion! I guess the reason I didn't want him is because I thought my parents would kill me. I wish I had known sooner how supportive they would be. . . .

June 21: Being pregnant is starting to annoy me. I have forgotten what it's like *not* to be pregnant, which is a definite indication that I need to have the baby *now*! My apprehension about being a good mother is a lot smaller now; I look at other people and see them do things I'd *never* do, which makes me think I'll do okay just out of instinct. And me and Scott talk about what we'd do in certain situations all the time. I may get scared again when he's born, but for now I'm actually kind of confident that I can be a great mom! And I have no doubt that Scott will be an excellent father. . . .

June 27: Today is just one of those days when I feel pretty good physically, but I want to kill someone. I am so tired of being pregnant! . . . I want to lie on my stomach again. I want to go swimming. I want to smoke a pack or two of Marlboro Reds in a single day! Argh!!!! . . .

The Pregnancy Goes On . . . and On . . . and On

July 5: Yesterday Scott and I had a highly emotional yet much-needed experience. He was asleep, and I took his wallet in the bathroom (so I could turn a light on) to get $20 out for birth announcements. When I opened it, a condom fell out. This was a problem because (1) we hardly ever have sex, and (2) since I'm pregnant we no longer use condoms. I went back in my room, huddled under the covers with my back to him, and cried silently. When Scott woke up, he immediately noticed that I was ignoring him and asked what was wrong. When I told him, he said it was his brother's, and I said that's exactly what a guilty person would say. He got mad and started yelling, which made me cry again. I said, "How am I not supposed to get upset?" but it came out in one of those sobbing voices, and then I just got hysterical. It was the first time I can think of that I let myself get like that in front of him. He went crazy! He jumped back on the bed and held me until I calmed down, then we talked about it and it was okay. I've never been so sure he loves me as I am after that!

July 7: 35 weeks today! I can't believe how quickly it has passed by. But now the time has slowed down, and every day seems like a hundred years. . . .

July 8: I have the strangest feeling that I'm going to have the baby. Physically. I can't explain it; I just feel like I'm going to have him soon! . . .

July 16: A lot has happened concerning me, Scott, and the baby. First of all, Scott has quit his job. He met a guy who sells insurance, and he went for an interview. Then he and the guy went out for a day so Scott could see what he would be doing. He really thinks he's going to like it. Problem is, he has to go to a training school in Nashville (2 hours away) for 3½ weeks. We followed his mom down there on Sunday (12th), and I rode back with her. He gets to come home on the weekends, and of course if I go into labor, but other than that I have to go the whole time without seeing him! I haven't seen him in 4 days; the longest we have been apart in our whole relationship. I can't eat, I can't sleep, and I haven't even gotten dressed. This sucks. I really really didn't want him to go, but I couldn't help it. This job is exactly what we need. . . .

July 20: The baby dropped last week. I noticed that my stomach looked different, and after a few tests realized that I no longer suffer from shortness of breath! . . . When the baby moves his head, it feels like someone is twisting my pelvic bone in half, and sometimes I even feel like I'm about to pee in my pants! But I am very glad that this pregnancy is almost over!

Yesterday we took Scott back to Nashville. Unless (1) I go into labor or (2) I convince someone to take me all the way down there for a visit, I won't get to see him again until August 3. We had a really great weekend together though. . . .

July 24: The past few days have been pretty terrible as far as the pregnancy goes. I cannot get comfortable enough to fall asleep at night, and just when I do, I have to get up and use the bathroom. Also, I tend to alternate between my left and right sides at night to keep my shoulders from being sore, but the pressure on my pelvic joints makes it nearly impossible to roll over. I have two pillows under my head, one between my knees, one under my belly, and one extra one. It's a good thing I have a full-sized bed! Needless to say, I haven't been in a very good mood this week. . . .

On the Eve of the Change from Teen to Teen Mom

July 26: I am *so very* pissed off! A girl posted on one of the teen pregnancy message boards I visit, asking what the other teen moms had decided as far as breast vs. bottle. I wrote her back, telling her that I am planning to bottlefeed and why. (In case you want to know, it's because I'll be going back to school in October). . . . I . . . wished her good luck with her own decision, and this bitchy girl replied to my post. She told me how terrible I was for deciding to bottlefeed, and how my baby would get sick and die if I didn't breastfeed, and that it's a baby's "birthright" to be breastfed. How is she going to sit there and say those things to me? . . .

July 27: Forget being mad; I am the happiest person on the planet! Scott called, and he gets to come home the day after tomorrow! I'm so excited. The days I've had to go without him have been absolutely terrible for me, especially with my constant fear of going into labor and him not making it home in time. I'm actually kind of nervous; my stomach has gotten noticeably bigger since I saw him last, and I'm scared he'll think I'm *huge*! But at the same time, I know he doesn't think of me as "fat." Because every time I say something about being ready to lose all this weight and get skinny again, he says, "Look, you are not fat. You are carrying *our son* inside of you, and that is nothing to be ashamed of. That makes it beautiful." *I love my boyfriend!!!* . . .

August 3: Well, I've been in early labor for over 75 hours and I'm still not even in the hospital. And Scott went back to Nashville a few hours ago; he won't be able to come home until he gets done with his last classes, so if I have the baby before the evening of the 6th, he won't get to be there. He's really upset about it, and so am I! I'm having back labor, which is probably the most painful experience of my life, but the contractions are not too bad right now. I just wish this baby would get out of me! . . . I'm so tired; I can't even sleep because of the constant aching in my lower back. *This sucks!* . . .

August 4: Things have been so hectic around here I haven't even had a chance to sit and think. Can this really be one of the last days before I go from "pregnant" to "parent"? Is it possible that the life inside of me is the size of a newborn baby? It's so hard to imagine! I feel huge, but I know that I'm tiny compared to most people at 39 weeks. Looking down at my belly (how I would love to see my feet!), it doesn't seem like it's possible for my child to be in there still. And now that I'm so close to having him, I'm really not so sure I want to! I'm going to miss feeling his wiggles, kicks, and stretches. I'm going to miss people asking me questions, even the annoying ones. I can't believe I'll wake up one morning soon and be able to roll over onto my stomach or jump out of bed without cringing in pain, but at the same time I'm not sure I want to. Most of all, I'm going to miss my old life. Never again will it be just me and Scott, coming and going with reckless abandon, staying out late with our friends, lying on the couch watching movies. Now we'll be Mommy and Daddy, giving bottles and baths, changing diapers and baby clothes, wishing we could just go to sleep. It's going to be one of the hardest transitions we've ever had to go through in our relationship, and I'm scared. . . . I didn't realize how fast things were about to change, or how much. I just hope I can handle it when the time comes. . . .

Motherhood and Insecurity

September 2: I'm a mom! It's such a dramatic change. . . . Sometimes I don't get a chance to brush my teeth until 3 or 4 in the afternoon, I only get to take a shower every other day (unless I get lucky and someone watches the baby for awhile), and the amount of sleep I get in a week is less that I used to get in one night. It gets so frustrating to sit at home when everyone else is out. . . . But at the same time, I love my son and I can live with the changes. Scott is so crazy about him! He is such a great father, just like I knew he'd be. . . .

September 3: Me and Scott had a long, calm discussion about some problems we've been having, and I think everything will be okay. A lot of it is the fact that I'm *extremely* insecure about his feelings for me. I can't help it—it is almost impossible for me to believe that someone could really care for me and love me. But I believe he does. . . . In a small way I wish we could get married now. It would be better for Jayden to have one home with both parents, but right now we can't afford a house. And I couldn't handle being a wife, mother, *and* a student at age 15. But I am 100% sure I will never want anyone else.

September 21: I spent the night with Scott a few nights ago and we got into this huge fight. Finally I couldn't stand it anymore, and I went into his room to apologize. I told him why I was unhappy, why I'd been such a bitch, and what I thought we should do to fix it. We were lying in bed talking, and he said the most shocking thing I could have ever imagined! Somehow the future had come up, and he said, "Well, I won't lie to you. I want to marry you so bad I can't stand it! I know you're not ready, but I think about it all the time." *I couldn't believe it!* Ever since then I've been thinking a lot about us, and I really want to get married! Most of my reluctance was thinking *he* didn't want to. . . .

September 23: I swear, I couldn't be more confused if I tried. Scott is really jumping into things without talking to me. He can't manage money, he can't make up his damn mind, he doesn't even take time to realize there are two of us in this relationship. He announced yesterday that he's building our house right beside his mom and dad. Sorry to appear ungrateful (they would be giving us the land), but I *do not* want them breathing down my neck. I don't understand why sometimes he can be so wonderful and other times he is such a mindless asshole.

What am I supposed to do? Argh! Don't get me wrong—I love Scott with all my being. I want us to be together for the rest of our lives. But sometimes I get so frustrated because he does things to mess up what we have. I can't trust him; I can't believe a word he says. Half the time I'm not even sure I believe that he cares about me. I do, however, see that he's trying to change for me and that he wants me, Jayden, and himself to stay together as a family. I'm just so confused! . . .

October 20: Oh my gosh, I am so happy and excited! A few days ago I thought I heard Scott talking to his mom about getting me an engagement ring. . . . He's going to ask me to marry him! I can't believe it! He is really going to propose to me, ask me to spend the rest of my life with him, make our relationship permanent! I just can't get over this. I never thought the day would come when I would be faced with such a giant decision. Of course I'm going to accept, but there is so much responsibility involved. I'm only 15 years old. The rest of my life is a *long* time! . . .

Marriage: A Very Big Commitment

October 26: Things continue to be okay between us, but I wish Scott would be more responsible. He's been better about spending time with Jayden, but he acts like he'd die if he had to go one night without going out. Even when he stays the night, he goes out for a few hours before he comes here to stay. He isn't paying any of the bills, and he sits on his butt while I juggle homework *and* the baby. It makes me *so* mad! I don't know what to do about it though. I don't want to start another family argument.

November 2: On the marriage front . . . I'm starting to freak out. What if we get married and he does or says something totally unforgiveable? Or what if we have a huge fight and can't [stand] each other? What if he cheats on me? I am so paranoid; I'm not sure I can deal with such a big commitment. . . .

November 6: Jayden will be 3 months old tomorrow! It just doesn't seem like it's been that long. He is getting so smart! . . .

November 17: Scott told me last night that he got the ring. I'm glad I don't have to be so quiet about it now! We talked a lot about marriage, and July 24 (the day we met) is on a Saturday next year so we may set the date for then. Of course, it is going to be *hard,* being a wife at 16, but I think (hope) I can handle it. It's a responsibility I want. But then again, I need to be *absolutely* sure it's what I want. Because neither of us believes divorce is right. I'm so happy, but I'm also scared. I've grown up faster than I wanted to, and I'm afraid this will be a bigger step than I can handle. . . .

November 23: I'm not sure if I can marry Scott or not. I mean, I love him, but his family is driving me insane! I'm sick of them trying to run our lives and raise our child. I wish they would all just leave us alone and let us learn for ourselves.

December 18: The last day (at school) before Christmas Break is so unfair. All these people are getting cards and gifts from their friends, and all of us teen moms are getting ignored. As if we don't celebrate the holidays anymore since we've got kids. . . .

December 31: I am *officially* engaged to be married! It isn't really any different, but now we're planning the wedding (which is *strange*) and sometimes Scott just gives me this look that says "Hey, you're only months away from being my wife." It's one of the greatest feelings in the world!

On Christmas morning Jayden did three new things: he rolled from belly to back for the first time, he held his bottle all by himself, and he tried his hardest to crawl. I guess that's my present from him! It's so hard to believe he's almost five months old already! In such a short time frame, he's eating baby food and rolling around and grabbing his feet. . . . He's growing up way too fast for me! . . .

"I Hate My Life Sometimes"

February 13, 1999: Life has been completely nuts since I last wrote. I turned 16 on February 2. Jayden was in the hospital February 3–6 with RSV, respiratory synctial virus. Now he's much better, but I was one scared mommy when Scott showed up at school to sign me out, saying he had been admitted to the hospital! While he still can't quite sit up on his own, Jayden has become a world expert at rolling off couches, beds, and other elevated surfaces. It's not like I leave him on my bed and go out of the room; all his accidents happen when I'm sitting right beside him for some reason. . . .

Scott and I have decided to postpone wedding plans until the summer of 2000, when things will be more organized and we'll have more money saved up. It was hard not to get excited when I got my ring, but I'm glad we're waiting. We've been together for a year and a half, but that doesn't mean we're ready for marriage.

Parenthood has gotten more tolerable, but not necessarily easier. Scott and I have worked out a system for eating, smoking, getting the baby to sleep, etc. without killing each other. And I've gotten really good at doing homework and bottle-holding at the same time. But it makes me so mad to sit at home and miss ball games, movies, etc. while everyone else is out having fun. My friend Katrina (I don't think I've mentioned her before) is the only person I can talk to. Her son, Austin, was born the day after Jayden. . . . I hate my life sometimes.

I Lost My Son to My Parents

Samantha, as told to Anrenée Englander

The following selection is taken from Anrenée Englander's book *Dear Diary, I'm Pregnant: Teenagers Talk About Their Pregnancy.* Here, nineteen-year-old Samantha recounts how she was raped when she was fifteen, gave birth to a son, and then lost custody of the child to her parents. Although she understood that as a parent she was responsible for her child, Samantha explains, she was not mature enough to change her lifestyle and assume total accountability for her actions. After being asked to care for their grandson for increasingly long periods of time, Samantha reveals, her parents became so attached to the child and so disapproving of her actions that they sued for custody—and won. She describes her anguish at losing her son and documents the changes she has been making in her life in hope of proving herself mature enough to assume full responsibility for her child.

I'm nineteen, I'm already a mother. My son's name is Daval. He's three years old. It's a crazy story. He's a child that shouldn't have been born.

I was fifteen turning sixteen. I was walking home from swimming class, like I always did. There's a walkway that you have to walk along to get to my house. I'd walked that path so many times, it's not like I was scared or thought that anything was going to happen to me. I was just walking home. I was wearing my Walkman.

I remember my head getting hit, and then hitting the ground. That's about all I remember. I never saw him. At first I thought I got robbed, because my Walkman was gone. When I got up I was feeling a lot of pain. When I got home I clued in. I knew what happened when I went into the bathroom. There was a lot of blood and a lot of scratches on my face. I waited for a while and then I started to cry. A lot. I sat on the edge of the bathtub. My sister came in after a while. She looked to me and whispered, "What happened?" I started to cry. She looked at me and whispered, "Who did this to you?" I didn't answer. She asked me again. I just kept crying. Finally, with my nods and stuff, I guess, she figured it out.

Making Decisions

I found out I was pregnant four months afterwards. I didn't know what being pregnant felt like. I just thought it was because of the stress. The rape itself was a nightmare. To find out I was pregnant now just meant it hadn't ended.

They said, "You're pregnant," and I said, "OK, I'm going to kill it." To me it wasn't a child, it was an alien. Devil Spawn. That's the way I thought of it. I had no sympathy, I was going to kill it. I don't believe in abortion in my life. I don't believe in it as a means of birth control. If its life and death, then I believe in it. I believe rape is life and death. I was supposed to have an abortion, but with my body, if I'd had an abortion, I wouldn't have been able to have kids again and that would make me feel really terrible. I'm the kind of person that is very giving and very loving and I wanted to have a child that I could give everything to. That was my belief and that was my feeling. It was a very hard decision based on the fact that I was still at home, living with my parents, and basically it was, "I have this child or I never have kids again." People said I was too young, but I thought I was mature enough to make that decision, so I did.

My parents were like, "You're not having this child." They were really upset. Extremely. My mother wouldn't talk to me. My father was constantly down my throat because of it, and finally one day I just said, "Look, I'm leaving." I went to a shelter for quite a while. I have a cousin who was already at the shelter. My dad would send me money.

I was in school up until they told me I couldn't go. I was eight and a half months pregnant. I was going to therapy three times a week with the school counsellor. I hadn't talked to anyone, so it was good to talk. I accepted that I was pregnant and I was going to have this child. I thought about adoption, but to carry a child for nine months and then go through labour, you can't go through that and then give it away.

Reality Sets In

When he was born, I flipped. He was half white! I'm not a racist person, don't get me wrong, but I didn't expect it. I didn't know the rapist was white until my son was born. It shocked me. I definitely didn't expect that. Four hundred years of pain of black people and white people. I'm very well educated on my black history, and I'm proud of it. And I got raped by a white man, and I was pissed. Royally pissed.

For the first three days I didn't even want to look at him, I was so angry. I refused to breast-feed. I wouldn't hold him. I think what worked was, the day I got home I had an appointment with my psychiatrist. She sat me down and said, "You can blame this three-day-old baby for what happened four hundred years ago, or what happened nine months ago, or you can look at him and realize that half of him is you. Half of that baby is you." So it was like a shot of reality.

It took a while, but the first smile, the first wink, the first laugh, the first giggle . . . you start watching this child do things, you're amazed. If you sit and watch the child for twenty minutes, that's real entertainment. It's a mind-blow. He turned out to be a pretty cute kid, too. He had blue eyes and reddish-brown hair. He was beautiful.

When he was about two months old, he woke me up one morning. He was hungry, but he was quiet about it. He wasn't screaming or whining or anything. He was just in his crib babbling. So I went over. I looked over the side of the crib and he looked up at me and started smiling and laughing, and I thought, "Ohhhh, you're so cute." From that day he was my child. Definitely my child. He was my prized possession. Still is.

A Lot of Responsibility

Everybody thinks it's cool to have kids: "Oh, you got a little baby." But it's not like a doll or anything like that. It's a lot of responsibility. It's really difficult. You've got to rely on a lot of different people. If a teenager comes to me now and tells me they could do it on their own, they're crazy, because it's very difficult, financially, mentally and emotionally.

I think I had it harder than a lot of other mothers because of questions like, "Who's the father?" and you're like . . . I don't know. It's not like I can pinpoint one person and say, "He's the father." Another thing staged a large problem for me because it posed a lot of questions for a lot of people. They'd say, "He's half white. Why? Who's the father?" And then you can't say, "Well, the father is a rapist." At that point I think, "What am I going to tell this child when he is older? What am I going to say to him?" I don't know what to say to him. When he's older and says, "Who's my father?" I don't know what to say. You can't explain that to a child. It would crush a child.

After Daval was born, my parents still weren't talking to me. So basically I had the shelter, aunts and uncles that did a great job, friends and stuff like that. I just tried to maintain sanity. I still hadn't quite gotten rid of my gung-ho youth, my wild side. I still wanted to do all the things that I did before: getting into fights, just hanging out. That's what I wanted to do, but I had this child. I know a lot of people thought negative of it and one actually thought it was pretty stupid that I continued to do what I always wanted to do. I'm a very strong-headed person. There were a lot of different events where people would say they were going to call a child protection agency on me because I wasn't a good enough mother. Basically I told them to go stick their nose somewhere else, to put it politely. And I didn't really care.

It got to a point where I wasn't mistreating him, I wasn't beating him or not taking care of him, but one time it was two o'clock in the morning and I'm outside with a baby stroller and people were looking at me like I was crazy. I took care of him but still wanted to do what I wanted to do, and I think that was very wrong of me, very selfish. I was mature, but I wasn't mature enough to know that the responsibility of a child is a lot more than having him, feeding him, changing him and that's it. There's a lot more to it. You have to give your child respect. You don't have a two-month-old, three-month-old, even two-year-old baby out at two o'clock in the morning. There's no reason for that. A child needs to feel protected at all times. You can't do that when you're downtown, outside, and around people who are smoking or doing whatever else.

"My Mother Now Has My Son"

My mom used to say, "Once you have a child, your life is over and their life begins. You're living your life to make your child's life better," and I wasn't doing that. I was still trying to live my life at the same time. You can live your life, but your life is supposed to change. You're supposed to grow more mature and pay more attention to your responsibilities, and I wasn't doing that.

He started to walk. That was the good news. He started to walk and babble and laugh. I had my own place. Things got a lot better. I was working. My parents were more trusting, more compassionate towards me. They would help with the baby-sitting.

I stayed with Daval for about a year, then I started working again. I'd give him to my parents. They'd take him. Then things started to get really hard. I started working longer hours to afford where I was living and to afford to buy clothes. So he spent more time at my parents' house, which my mother loved. She got more attached to him. Basically he was living at my parents' house because I was working hours that I was up at seven-thirty A.M. to get to work for ten A.M. I'd work all hours of the night, until all the work was done. We'd close at nine-thirty P.M., then it would take about one hour to count the money and restock the shelves. So basically I was seeing my child about three hours a day, and my mother didn't approve of that. That went on until he was about two. But I couldn't quit my job. I was trying to pay bills, support him with money—have money to do the things . . . give him the things he deserves. By the time I realized that something was wrong, it was too late. . . . About three weeks after he turned two and a half, [my mother] told me, "I'm taking him from you." And I was just like, "What do you mean?"

Now, my parents are well off. My parents have it made. I can't say that it was handed to them on a silver platter, because it wasn't. They worked really hard to get it, but they've got it now. My parents could give him anything he wanted. He could say he wanted a car and my parents could give it to him, and I couldn't do that. Well, it became one really big court battle, and my mother pulled up dirt that I never even knew that she knew. The child protection agency got involved.

Basically, the moral of the story is, I lost my son to my parents. The court took away something that was mine. He was part of me. My mother now has my son. She's had him for about six months. I have no contact with them at all. My mother and I don't speak. We can't stand each other. I won't subject my child to fistfights. I won't let him see violence. And if me and my mother are in the same room, there'll be violence. I'd kill her if she put her hands on my child. And if my child calls her "mother," that's even worse. My child's old enough to know who I am. I'm sure he loves me.

"Everything I Do Is to Get Him Back"

Emotionally, it turned me right off, to the point where I started drinking heavily, getting into drugs, I wouldn't go in to work, I wouldn't sleep. I was trying to fill up that hole of emptiness that was there. Emotionally, I was unstable. Physically, I was unstable because I wasn't taking care of myself. Mentally, I was definitely unstable. My outlook on life—there was none. I didn't know what I was doing wrong or what I was supposed to do. I felt lost, because this is the child my parents didn't want me to have and now my mother has taken him from me, and emotionally I was just confused. I didn't think it was fair.

My cousin, we've been the best of friends. One day she said to me, she actually grabbed me by the back of my head and said, "Look, you can't change the past, but it's not going to do you any good to go on the way you have." She explained to me that my mother's old. "There's going to be a day when your mother won't be able to take care of him and you're going to get him back." Every day when I wake up, I strive to get him back. Everything I do is to get him back. If I see a pair of baby shoes or a sweater, I'll buy it, I'll put it aside for him. I work towards getting him back.

Mentally, I think I'm more stable than I've been in my whole entire life. Physically, I'm very healthy, I take care of myself. And emotionally, because of my cousin and a lot of other people, I've been able to regain what I once had. What I do now is just try and work towards getting him back, and that's probably the biggest dream I've ever had. People have dreams: they want to be doctors, nurses, athletes and whatever. I work towards getting him back. He was my life.

A Dysfunctional Family Life

I wasn't taught right from wrong. My parents are more corrupt than I am, actually. I have a very weird tale about my birth. My older sister is my mother. She had me a year and a half after her first child. I thought he was my nephew, but actually he's my brother. She could not handle having two, so she gave me to her mother. When I was five years old, the adoption papers were signed. So my mother and father are actually my grandparents, and I think that has the biggest twist ever. I only found out when I was eighteen. I went hysterical. I actually did freak out.

From kindergarten to Grade 7 everything was fine. Once I hit Grade 8, I don't know what happened. I fell into the wrong crowd. I wanted to be like everyone else. My mother was very strict. She forbid me to do just about anything that was fun. My mother was abusive. Her way of disciplining was to knock you out. There's never been anything extreme that I've done, that I can remember, but I can remember getting hit for it. My parents used things like extension cords, belt buckles, venetian blind cords, shoes, metal spoons. I just started getting ruthless and reckless, and did I ever get into trouble for it.

I think from birth we didn't like each other. She never really considered me as her child. I don't believe that I was ever accepted. It's something I've always thought—the attitude that I didn't really belong—and when I found that I wasn't even a part of that family, it kind of clicked. My family are professional liars. They're great at covering things up. I try not to dwell on it. I guess I'm in denial: "Oh, it's no big deal, who cares?" And I just leave it at that.

What hurts is not really knowing who my real father is. My sister won't tell me. She thinks that I don't need to know and I think that's why we don't talk. It's affected my life in such a big way that I want to know. Because of the fact that I've lost my son, I don't talk to my mother and I don't talk to my sister. I don't really talk to many people. I feel like I can't trust everybody else. You're lied to and then your child is stolen away from you. To me, it seems like there's this really big plan, this big plot. I really believe that they want to see me fail.

I am now a manager with the same company that I was with before. It's a retail company. I run fifteen different stores. It's fun. I work hard and save. I put it away. I have my own apartment. And I'm alive! It's easier now than it was before, when I first lost him. Now I enjoy life. Maybe if my family would come and visit me . . . but I take that in stride. When I'm ready, I'm going to go back into the courts and say, "I want my child back. Look, I've got this, I've done this, I've done that. I want my child back. I deserve to have my child back. He deserves to be with me. Nobody knows him better. Nobody can raise him better."

I think I'm waiting till I'm done being a kid. Everyone thinks of me as an adult, and in some aspects I am. I've got money and I'm stable, but I'm not done being a kid. That's what I'm waiting for. We go from child to adult. There's nothing in between. It'll happen. I think it might even happen this year. When I'm ready I'll know.

Stopping the Cycle of Teen Pregnancy

I'm doing this interview because I know I'm not the only teen mom out there. There are a lot of girls out there who feel lost. And there are a lot of teen mothers out there who've lost their children and are in that rut that I was in, and they can't seem to find their way out. I sympathize with them. Emotionally, I can feel their pain. It feels like the world is coming down on them.

I also know how hard it is to take care of a child. I'm doing this to show people that it's not the end of the world and there is a way out. There is a light at the end of the tunnel. The way I see it, keep strong and work towards a goal. If you make a goal and you work towards that goal, you feel a lot better when you get there. Everyone has the ability to do everything they want. I'm not telling teenagers to go out and have kids, because that would be wrong. I know how difficult it is. If you have one, your whole life is supposed to change. There's no more parties, no more guys, no more hanging out with the friends. All that changes because you have a child. That child has to go everywhere you go. You have to concentrate mostly on that child. To those teenagers who want kids, I tell them, sit back and think about it, because it's tough. Why take away youth? There's plenty of time. There's no reason to jump into it and have them right now. If you're financially stable, if you've got the money to do it, then by all means, but most people aren't. Actually, 99.9 percent of us aren't.

Teenagers that actually have kids at this point, all I can say is: Keep your head up, keep trying. Keep working hard at it, because it all pays off. It really does, when your child turns around and says, "I love you, Mom." When your child is sixteen or seventeen, the age we are now, you can sit down with your child and talk to them. Stop the cycle that's been going on for the longest time: teenagers having children. The way I see it, it's up to our generation to stop that cycle. More and more every day you hear about ten- and twelve-year-olds having kids, and that's ridiculous. For a sixteen-year-old to have a child—it's ridiculous. I think it's up to our generation to stop it. We have the biggest weapon right now, and that's our kids. If we can raise our children and teach them right from wrong from the very start, then the world will be a better place.

THREE TEEN MOMS WHO BEAT THE ODDS

Alexis Sinclair

Many teen mothers find it difficult, if not impossible, to achieve their dreams and give their children the type of life they would like them to have. However, some teen mothers do realize their goals despite the odds. In the following article, Alexis Sinclair interviews three young mothers who were still in their teens when they had their babies twelve years earlier. All three women kept their children and, at one point in time, each chose to become a single parent. During the interview, each woman describes the circumstances surrounding her pregnancy and the decisions and sacrifices she made over the years to help ensure her future and that of her child. Sinclair is a freelance writer who contributes to such magazines as *Cosmopolitan*, *Redbook*, and *Working Mother*.

Being a mom isn't easy. Witness the undereye circles of the woman who was up at 3:00 A.M. to nurse her teething baby. Now imagine coping with those demands when you're only a teenager. It may seem like an insurmountable challenge, but these three tough young mothers never gave up.

From Scared and Abused Mom to Successful Model
Sonia McDaniel: I was a good girl from Colorado Springs: 17 years old, quiet, responsible, a cheerleader. Clint, 22, was my first boyfriend; we met when I was working at Wendy's after school. After dating only a few months, we took off to San Diego, the city he'd grown up in. He told me he loved me, and I blindly went for it. Plus, I saw it as a chance to rebel against my "too good" image.

Within a year, I was pregnant. We were living with Clint's grandmother while I finished high school and he worked for a landscaper. After the initial shock, Clint and I were actually exalted. I wanted to be a mom, and it seemed like the perfect next step in our relationship. My mother was also excited when I told her (she bragged that at 37, she'd make a good-looking grandma). I guess I knew deep down,

Reprinted from Alexis Sinclair, "Against All Odds: Three Teenage Moms 12 Years Later," *Cosmopolitan*, November 1998. Reprinted with permission from the author.

though, that Clint wouldn't make a good husband, because when he proposed, I didn't say yes.

When Christina was born, I thought Oh, wow. She's a real baby. I'd sit for hours and stare at her. Our daughter was so adorable: a strawberry blond, mellow child. Maybe because I'd baby-sat for all my 12 younger cousins so often, I felt very prepared to be a mother. But I hadn't braced myself for living with an abusive boyfriend.

When Christina was 2 months old, Clint became very controlling— he wouldn't let me leave the house, he monitored my calls; once, he even chased me up the street in his car. Clint also told me he had an incurable disease—that he was dying. But since he had no symptoms, what that meant didn't really sink in. So there I was, living with an abusive, sick boyfriend with a baby—but not without a plan.

One day, he was remorseful after a huge fight (during which he'd broken my nose), so I sweet-talked him into letting me take Christina shopping. (Usually, when I went out, he insisted that Christina stay with him—she was insurance that I would come back.) I drove us straight to a shelter with only the clothes on our backs.

I was 22, had moved to Las Vegas, and was renting my first apartment. I was also working like a dog at a construction company while I took evening classes to get my degree in business administration. During the day, Christina went to day care, and at night, I'd study and try to play with her. I had no life, but I kept at it until I graduated with a 3.5 grade point average.

My big break came four years ago [in 1994], when I became a Penthouse Pet by landing a centerfold. I'd always wanted to model and nudity is not something I'm ashamed of. Suddenly, I was signing autographs and even had my picture taken with Fabio. (I sent it to my aunt!) And I also started doing fashion modeling. My only fear was that Clint would resurface, but I've since learned that he died from his illness.

Now, the hardest thing is dealing with a pubescent 11-year-old daughter. When it comes to major crises, I've learned to stay calm and look to Christina for solace—I've had to after 11 years of making big decisions and occasional mistakes all by myself.

From Shelter Dweller to Music-Biz Whiz

Rece Walford: I knew even without a test that I was pregnant—I was sick and gaining weight. But I didn't want to deal with it and hoped it would just magically go away. I was 16 and more or less on my own— technically, I was in the custody of my dad, but he lived at his girlfriend's most of the time, and I hadn't lived with my mom since I was taken from her when I was 6 (she had suffered a nervous breakdown). The father of my baby, Joe, was a good friend I had known since we were 13. He'd spend the weekends at my house. Like clockwork, I would arrive home from my night job at McDonalds, and he'd be there.

I started to show at three or four months—that's when I became depressed and started cutting school. I didn't really make a conscious decision to keep the baby—I think partly because I didn't have a mom around to tell me what to do and partly because I was in denial.

I told Joe I'd deal with the pregnancy on my own. I'd always been self-reliant, plus I found out that Joe was dealing drugs. The decision was fine with him, and he dropped out of my life. (He is now in prison, where may son visits him every so often.) I felt I had let my father down, so my aunt insisted that I move in with her and finish school. For that, I was grateful: I was four months pregnant, lonely, and terrified.

Daymond was born prematurely at seven months, weighing just over four pounds. He was the tiniest thing I'd ever seen. I loved Daymond fiercely, but there were times when I wanted to be the kid. I did not know how to handle the frustration of being 16 and expected to act like a mature adult. That conflict made me resentful at times. Those first months were tough with school and work and the tiny baby, but I stuck to my guns—I was determined to make a good life for us. I went to school, then worked at the Gap from 4:00 P.M. to 1:00 A.M. I was reeling from exhaustion, but I did it. I graduated within a year, in the summer of 1989. Daymond was just 2.

At 17, I moved out of my aunt's house and enrolled in a work/living program in New York City at a shelter called Covenant House. I stayed there and did job training and eventually got a staff position as an assistant with Guardian Life Insurance.

I wanted the very best for Daymond, so I put him in private school to give him every opportunity to excel. But in exchange, we've had to sacrifice in other areas of our lives. After I left the program, for example, the only apartment I could afford was a crack-infested dump in the Bronx. Preparing to move in, I sat in the U-Haul out in the rain, slumped over the steering wheel, crying. That's when I decided we deserved a better life. Children grow up identifying with their neighborhoods, and Daymond was entitled to a nurturing atmosphere. I turned the truck around and rented a house in Queens with another single mom.

I imagine there are plenty of things I could've done if I hadn't had a baby—like go to the prom (for starters), have freedom, follow my dream of acting—but I also know that where I am right now is exactly where I am meant to be. Daymond has taught me to take responsibility and to make choices with our future in mind. My career in insurance had taken me as far as I could go, for instance, so I decided to find work in the music industry. I pounded the pavement and finally got a job at Motown A&R as a production coordinator. On the side, I worked freelance on music videos with stars like L.L. Cool J, Brandy, and director Hype Williams. Now, here I am, working in the licensing division at BMG Entertainment (a top 10 entertainment company

that owns record labels like Arista), renting a nice two-bedroom apartment in New York City, and raising an incredibly smart and sweet 11-
year-old boy. The sacrifices are hard (I haven't been on a date in
months!), but I'm proud that I can offer Daymond the support and
stability that I never had. He is my inspiration.

From Desperate Divorcée to Medical Student

Kara Pattinson: I was 18 and naive. I thought that if you loved someone, you married him. That's why it was easy for me to give up my
dream of becoming a doctor for the love of a man.

His name was Tim, and he was in the Air Force. We met in San
Diego, where I was going to college. Six months later, we got hitched
before a justice of the peace, just like that, without telling anyone.
Tim was black, and I knew the interracial aspect wouldn't go down
well back home. In fact, later, when my grandparents found out about
us, they immediately disowned me.

Six months later, I was pregnant. My mother, who lived in Eugene,
Oregon, said I was ruining my life. I, on the other hand, was thrilled
because I really wanted children. A few months into my pregnancy, I
left school and joined Tim in Okinawa, Japan, where he had been stationed. That's where Alex was born.

The delivery was a horrible, painful, two-day ordeal that ended
with an infected incision from my C-section. The following month
was extremely difficult: I suffered severe postpartum depression. All I
could do was sit around and cry. It didn't help that I sensed Tim was
growing distant. During labor, he left the room like he didn't want to
deal with it. And when Alex was born, Tim refused to change his
lifestyle: He continued to stay out late with friends—and he wouldn't
help when the baby cried.

When Alex was a month old, we went to Oregon and spent a few
months with my mother. My depression slowly lifted, and for the first
time, I began to love being a mom—nursing, diapering, everything.
This time, my mother was behind me all the way. She really fell in
love with Alex. But when Alex and I joined Tim back in San Diego,
where he was then stationed, things returned to the way they'd been
overseas.

I was in a loveless situation, and I felt compelled to show Alex
there was more to life. So for the next few years, I waitressed and kept
the books at a gas station and eventually socked away enough money
to ask Tim for a divorce. He was floored but did not oppose it. At first,
I felt guilty about taking Alex from his dad. Then I discovered that
Tim had a girlfriend, and guess what? She was pregnant. That did it.

I desperately wanted to do something that would eventually give
Alex a better life. I'd sacrificed my professional future for love when I
moved to Japan, and now I dreamt of becoming a doctor. Honestly, at
that point, nothing seemed impossible. So evenings, I took prerequi-

sites at a community college and started on the right track. My sched-ule was crazy: I'd drop Alex off at school at 7:00 A.M. and pick him up at 6:00 P.M., then attempt to read him a book before we both passed out. Tim was not in the picture at all. Alex and I were a team—we bat-tled everything together.

This is my second year of med school and also the first year of my second marriage. I met my husband, Joshua, in biology class, and we were married in July 1998. Alex sees Tim (who lives with another woman and their two kids) once a year.

Given the chance, I would have done some things differently, but I've never for an instant regretted having Alex. If not for him, I would never have found the drive to get myself into medical school. We've formed a cement bond helping each other through tough times— we're each other's personal cheerleaders.

A Birthmother's Story

Kay Hagan-Haller

Having a child out of wedlock was less accepted a few decades ago than it is today, especially if the mother was still in her teens. In most cases, the pregnancy was kept a closely guarded secret, the mother-to-be was sent away from home until after she gave birth, and her child was placed for adoption. Kay Hagan-Haller underwent such an experience as a seventeen-year-old college student in the 1970s. According to the author, her boyfriend refused to accept responsibility for the pregnancy, and she checked into a home for unwed mothers. She describes her experiences at the home, including humiliating treatment by the staff and the intense pressures placed on her to give up her son. Now a married mother of five other children, she writes that she is still dealing with the emotional pain of having lost her first-born child.

I was 17 and a freshman in college when I met J. He was a junior and about 21. I thought I was getting a neat man. My high school sweetheart and I had stopped seeing each other a few months before and I was devastated. This was going to be wonderful. I told him when he pushed for sex that I did not want to get pregnant. He assured me that he would marry me if that happened. I told him that I did not want to *have* to get married.

He seemed to be pleased that I thought that way. After a few months of struggling about sex, he convinced me that I was the one with the problem . . . so I did it—once. I can't help but wonder now, why not birth control? It was never mentioned between us. He broke up with me a week later. What we did could not really be thought of as making love. I won't go into detail, but I did not think pregnancy would occur. J told me that I would not be capable of sex. I thought he knew what he was talking about.

About five months later, movement convinced me that I might be pregnant. I went to a free clinic near the college. The girl in front of me got her negative results in the waiting room. I was called into the office. From the date of my last period, we established that I would be

Excerpted from Kay Hagan-Haller, "This Is My Birthmother Story," www.geocities.com. Reprinted with permission from the author.

about five months pregnant. The lady gave me information about a home for unwed mothers about 100 miles away. It was a Florence Crittendon Home (FCH). I was told that if I went there, I would have to give the baby up for adoption.

I walked out of there in a shock. What was I going to do? I drove around for a couple of hours until I knew it would be time for J to be home from classes. I pulled up right behind him. We had "the conversation" at the top of the driveway. It was pretty basic. I said I was pregnant. He said I couldn't be from what we had done. I said I was pregnant. He said it could not be his. I said that he knew I was a virgin before him. I said I was pregnant. He said I could not trap him into marrying me. I said I didn't even like him and would not marry him. He told me to go to my parents. With that he walked down the driveway and into the house without looking back. I never saw him again.

I got into my car and drove my little VW bug around and around the city. I thought of suicide. Then I thought about how my family would feel when they learned that not only had I killed myself, but was also pregnant and killed my baby. Not me! I would not have an abortion . . . I would not kill my baby. I went back to school and called my brother. He said that he would stay at his house until I got there. I told him and he insisted that I go to our parents. I said that I would not tell them. When I was 12 and had never even held hands with a boy, my mom had told me not to come home if I ever got pregnant. I never forgot. My brother took me to Mom and Dad's. We told them. My dad got that hurt look on his face and demanded to know who the boy was. I refused to tell him. My mom wanted to know why I waited until it was too late. I had no answer for her. I was a 4.0 student in college. Barely 18, I had finished a year already and was half way through another. I had a bright future ahead of me. I had ruined it.

In Prison at the Crittendon Home

We checked into the Florence Crittendon Home. Within two weeks I was standing in my room unpacking my few clothes and books. I had two roommates. One was friendly and the other was withdrawn. Later I learned that when girls got close to delivery, they started to withdraw. It took too much to be nice to the new girls then. K was my roommate. She and S (who lived down the hall) had all of my information within an hour. You used an assumed name. You were not allowed to divulge where you were from. It turned out that K was from my hometown. The father of her baby was my best friend's (since third grade) ex-boyfriend. K had taken him from her and I had hated her for months—as only a teenage girl could hate someone she never met! We became really close. She got me a job in the kitchen. This was the coveted position. It was more work, but we were the chosen ones. The lady who ran the kitchen loved each of us and was the only one around who treated us with respect.

The director was a cruel woman who seemed to enjoy putting us down and enforcing stupid rules. There were girls there who had not finished school and were young enough to need supervision. The youngest was only 13! At 18 I felt as though I was in prison! I was not allowed to have any visitors without parental approval. We were allowed to go out with a buddy twice per week. We could not go to the fast-food place. We found a grocery store with a bakery! We stuffed ourselves with forbidden baked goods. We bought candy and smuggled it back into the house. We made elaborate plans to be sure someone was going out every day to replenish our candy stash. If we received a package in the mail, it had to be opened in the office and checked. Any sweets were confiscated. I was there over Thanksgiving and Christmas. No one could send me any holiday treats. I got one box and it was taken. On Christmas Day I was allowed to have one piece and share one with the others. The rest was thrown away. The entire routine was designed to keep us under control. We had to attend clinic each Monday in a dress without panties. We were told that this was to make it go more quickly. We toured the hospital one Monday and were made to dress the same as clinic day. This was humiliating.

The Social Workers (SWs) completed the job of brainwashing and destroying our self-esteem. I was not seen by my SW but once before my son was born. I remember lying awake at night worrying that she would not get to me and he would not have a family to go to. Standard talk from the SWs: You cannot give your baby what the baby deserves, and adoptive parents can. The baby will always be a baby born out of wedlock and not accepted. You will never find a husband willing to take on this child. Your parents will be embarrassed. You won't be able to finish school and get a good job to support the two of you. You won't be a good parent. This was the hot topic of conversation. Everything that a SW told a girl was repeated over and over again to everyone. I wonder why many birthmothers have so little self-esteem now?

We were told to purchase an outfit for the baby to wear home, including plastic pants, booties . . . the whole thing. My sister brought me a blanket that my mom had made for my niece. We somehow thought that this would give him something from our family. I never have asked if he had it when adopted. I didn't want to know.

The afternoon of January 5, which was a Sunday, I started having a strange discharge. I asked the nurse what it meant. She told me that it meant that I was not going to make it to my due date (which was still five weeks away). The next morning I awoke to cramps. I jolted awake! I was not supposed to have period cramps!!! I went to the bathroom and lost my mucous plug. I went to the nurse, who had been up all night with three girls in labor. She gave me a pad and told me to pack a suitcase. When the others went to the hospital, I would go to be checked. I went down to breakfast but could not eat. My roommate K was leaving that morning. She had delivered on Christmas Eve. I asked her to call my parents when she got home. The director would not call until after you delivered. They did not want parents in the way. She had to go to court that morning to sign papers. [Note: Only the girls that went through Catholic Charities had to go to court.] The director laughed at me and told me that she was sure I would be back.

Giving Birth

I left for the hospital about 9:00 A.M. All of the others were checked first. Finally it was my turn. In the dressing room I removed my pad and was horrified to see that the discharge was bloody. The midwife asked questions like when was my due date. She told me that I was having Braxton-Hicks contractions, not labor. She said that the baby was not in the birth canal; I was not effaced or dilated. I was supposed to be glad because it was too early for the baby to be born. I went back to FCH. The director gave me the "I told you so" look and speech. I went upstairs to rest after eating a piece of toast and drinking some orange juice. S came to check on me several times. I did not want to come down to lunch and refused her offer to get someone. After lunch she came back and insisted on getting some help. The secretary came up and asked how far apart the contractions were—she had been with me at the hospital and knew what I had been told. I said that I had not bothered to time them—why would I? She asked for an estimate. I said maybe 10 minutes. She told me to get my dress back on and we were going to the hospital. If this was not real labor, they needed to give me something. I said I would get up after the contraction. Before I got across the room, another one hit. She freaked out—I can still hear her saying, "I thought you said 10 minutes!"

We rushed to the hospital. She stopped a security guard and he radioed inside to tell them I was coming. They held the elevators. It was exciting to an 18-year-old who had never been in a hospital before and had watched *Medical Center* and *Marcus Welby, MD*, on TV. I was ushered into the exam room. Very quickly the midwife ran out with eight fingers held high. She had asked me no less than three times what I had been told that morning. Soon I was in a labor room. We had classes every Monday after clinic where we were taught about labor and birth. Lamaze [a method of natural childbirth] was new then—but we were promised that we did not have to have any drugs if we did not want them. I planned to do it without drugs (I have had five children since without any pain drugs!). The midwife on duty was not one I had met before. She inserted the IV and then told me that the meds she just gave me might make me nauseous. I was furious that she would give me anything without telling me first. I was already dilated to eight centimeters and had done that without *any-*

thing! And the fact that, along with pain, now I might throw up? I could have killed her. She kept telling me to turn on my left side. We had been told to find our most comfortable position. My back was mine and now I was being told I could not do that.

Finally, I was pushed into the delivery room. There were little green men on the ceiling and no one would look at them with me. I was really "spacey." I do not know what drugs I was given but I really had a buzz and was in no condition to help deliver a baby. I was told that the baby was in distress and that a doctor would be there to use forceps. Soon they were rushing out of the room. I asked what it was. The nurse started telling me about some drug she was giving me. *No! The baby!!* Oh, it is a boy, and they had to rush him to Neonatal Intensive Care because he was early and not breathing properly.

At 3:03 P.M. January 6, 1975, I delivered a baby boy that I named James Patrick Hagan. Another midwife showed up to stitch up my shredded bottom. It took her over an hour. No one ever did look at the ceiling for the green men. When I was taken to a room, I was lucky that another FCH girl (L) was there to room with. Two of the other girls had delivered, but the third was still in labor. S came to the hospital shortly after and had her baby that night, too. We were way down at the end of the hall away from the other mothers. To get to the nursery we had a long walk. L asked me to go with her to see her baby. I knew that my son was on another floor. I walked with her. Her baby was way in the back away from the others. It looked as though he was being kept away from the other babies. While walking back, I fainted in the hallway. I was on the ceiling watching everyone run to me and get me in a wheelchair. I have heard about out-of-body experiences; I guess this was one. I don't really know. When back in my room I was told that I had a fever and was dehydrated. I needed to drink lots of water. I was also told that I was not to go anywhere without a nurse. I could not leave the floor to go to see my son.

Going Home Alone

My parents came the next morning. My mom was so sorry that she had not been there for me, but no one called her until K got home that afternoon. FCH would not tell her anything when she called except that I had gone to the hospital. I wanted my mom to take me to see my son but she would not. She said that she could not stand to see that little baby hooked up to machines and know he was her grandson and then not take him home. Why didn't I make her go? I was trying so hard not to cause any more problems. I had hurt my parents so much, and I wanted to make the hurt go away. I thought I could. I had been told over and over that when it was all over, I would forget. I don't know who made up that lie. Obviously, they had never given birth. I kept asking nurses to check on him and tell me that he was okay.

Finally one nurse took me up to his floor. He looked so tiny! He had wires attached to his chest and then to machines. The nurses there were so wonderful. They explained that he needed oxygen but would be okay. He was small but would grow. I got to put my hands into the isolet and touch him. He had long fingers like his father (and me). He was a long, thin baby (just as I had been). I thought that he looked like his father. He was certainly darker skinned than I. They would not let me stay long because the nurse had to get back to the floor.

I remember asking the midwife why he had been born so early. She told me that I must have mixed up my dates. I told her she was crazy because I knew the date of my last period and the date of conception. Finally, she admitted that she did not know.

The morning that I was released, I got to go to his floor and hold him. I was so excited that I was shaking. When I arrived in the Neonatal Intensive Care Unit, I put on a gown and washed my hands. The nurse said that they planned to give him a bath in a few minutes so she pulled off the wires, wrapped him in a blanket and handed me a now-screaming baby. He and I looked into each other's eyes and he stopped crying. One nurse said, "Well, he sure knows his momma!" She was promptly kicked by the other nurse and I heard the whisper, "She's FCH. . . ." I held him as long as they would allow before I went back to my room. I left the hospital a few minutes later.

The midwife told me that I could go home on January 20. That was my dad's birthday. I missed my mom's on January 11. I begged and begged to go home early. No way. I spent my last two weeks at FCH crying. After you got back from the hospital you moved from your old room to Mother's Quarters. We were packed in because so many delivered so close together. We no longer had to do chores. We sat around and talked about our labors and what we would do when we got home. Girls who were still pregnant came to sit with us and ask questions about what it was like. We worried about our babies. We wondered if what we had been told was true.

One of the other girls explained to me that I could put a hold on my baby for 30 days so that I could get home and see if I could work something out to keep him. The SW finally sat down with me to fill out the papers. She asked me about the birthfather. I told her that he would deny being the father and there was no reason to talk to him at all. She told me that they had a young male SW who they sent and he would talk to him and J would probably sign the papers. I thought it would be a good idea to try just to get medical information. I knew his father had died young but not why. She had me fill out medical history. My dad had not yet had cancer or heart disease. My grandmother and aunt had not yet gotten glaucoma. We appeared very healthy on paper. I don't remember much else.

The day I left I signed the papers in the office by myself. I was 18. I could not sign a contract to buy a car or rent an apartment, but I could sign papers to give my baby to strangers. My parents were not present, no lawyer, not even the SW, only the secretary of FCH.

Life Goes On

I went home to find that if I wanted my job, I had to go back to work on Monday. That would be exactly three weeks postpartum. I did it, though. I thought that my insides would fall out after a couple of hours of standing. Everyone thought I had been sick, so my boss gave me a chair to use when there were no customers. Her boss was not impressed, so I used it only when I could no longer stand. I was supposed to have been in Florida with an aunt. I had no tan and had gained weight. I was not heavy but my hips were bigger and I never again got into the straight skirts I had worn. I just knew that people would *know* just by looking at me. One of the women with whom I worked had a daughter that was a year or two older than me. She had warned me about J when we were first dating. I did not want her to know she had been right. My boss had told me that if I acted like a lady, I would be treated like one. I guess I didn't act like a lady, huh?

I decided that I would not go back to school until I decided what I wanted to do since I no longer wanted to teach kindergarten. I worked and went home. I did so much want to find a man who would care about me! My self-esteem was at an all-time low. I thought about my baby constantly. I wondered if he was okay. I knew he had left the hospital the day after I did, but not where he went. I was so worried that he might not be healthy. The SW called to tell me that J had signed the papers. I was so happy that he finally admitted that he was the father. And now that he had signed away his rights, I knew he could not get his hands on my son. The SW started pressing me to release the baby from the hold I had placed. She told me that I would have to pay for the foster care by the day that he was there and his medical bills. I was terrified that after I paid that there would be no savings left to buy him clothes and food. I caved in and let him be adopted. I would regret that for the rest of my life.

I spent several years looking for something to fill that hole in my life. I dated many men. I drank. Nothing worked. I finally married and started a family. We have five children together. I love them all dearly but there is still a hole in my heart where my firstborn belongs.

ORGANIZATIONS TO CONTACT

The editors have compiled the following list of organizations concerned with the issues presented in this book. The descriptions are derived from materials provided by the organizations. All have publications or information available for interested readers. The list was compiled on the date of publication of the present volume; the information provided here may change. Be aware that many organizations take several weeks or longer to respond to inquiries, so allow as much time as possible.

Advocates for Youth

1025 Vermont Ave. NW, Suite 200, Washington, DC 20005
(202) 347-5700 • fax: (202) 347-2263
e-mail: info@advocatesforyouth.org
website: www.advocatesforyouth.org

Advocates for Youth's focus is on preventing pregnancy and sexually transmitted diseases among adolescents. Through its specialized clearinghouses on teen pregnancy prevention, school condom availability, peer education, school-based health centers, sexuality education, and adolescent reproductive health initiatives, the organization provides up-to-date information to educators, students, policy makers, and healthcare providers. Its numerous publications include the newsletters *Transitions* and *Advocates Alert* and the five-volume series *Communities Responding to the Challenge of Adolescent Pregnancy*.

Alan Guttmacher Institute (AGI)

120 Wall St., New York, NY 10005
(212) 248-1111 • fax: (212) 248-1951
e-mail: info@agi-usa.org • website: www.agi-usa.org

AGI works to protect and expand the reproductive choices of all women and men worldwide. The institute strives to ensure people's access to the information and services they need to exercise their rights and responsibilities concerning sexual activity, reproduction, and family planning. It conducts domestic and international projects designed to foster reproductive health, effective prevention of unintended pregnancy, the right to abortion, and societal support for parenting. Among the institute's publications are the book *Teen Pregnancy in Industrialized Countries*, the report "Sex and America's Teenagers," the bimonthly periodical *Family Planning Perspectives,* and the quarterly periodical *International Family Planning Perspectives*.

Alliance for Young Families

105 Chauncy St., Eighth Floor, Boston, MA 02111
(617) 482-9122 • fax: (617) 482-9129
e-mail: youngfamilies@bizhost.com
website: www.youngfamilies.org

A coalition of approximately one hundred health and human services agencies, Alliance for Young Families works to prevent teenage pregnancy, promote adolescent health, and meet the needs of teen parents and their children. The alliance's Teen Parent Policy Advisory Board consists of current and former teen parents who give presentations about teen pregnancy prevention and teen parent issues. The organization's publications include the reports "Living on the Edge: The Housing Crisis Facing Teen Parents and Their Children," "Teen Parent Day Care in Massachusetts: Helping Young Families Help Themselves," and "'I Had the Stress of the World': A Report on Young Fathers in Massachusetts."

Campaign for Our Children (CFOC)
120 W. Fayette St., Suite 1200, Baltimore, MD 21201
(410) 576-9015
website: www.cfoc.org

CFOC uses mass media advertising, media relations, school programs, and public health outlets to promote abstinence to adolescents. The organization produces educational videos, lesson plans, posters, television and radio ads, billboards, and brochures in English and Spanish. Among its publications are the brochure *Talking the Talk* and the educational sets "Abstinence Makes the Heart Grow Fonder" and "You Play, You Pay."

Child Trends (CT)
4301 Connecticut Ave. NW, Suite 100, Washington, DC 20008
(202) 362-5580 • fax: (202) 362-5533
e-mail: swilliams@childtrends.org (research inquiries)
website: www.childtrends.org

CT studies issues concerning children, youth, and families through research, evaluation studies, and data collection and analysis. The organization's many areas of interest include teenage pregnancy and parenting. CT publishes the annual newsletter *Facts at a Glance,* reports on specific research projects, a series of research briefs, and the papers "Piecing Together the Puzzle of Teenage Childbearing," "Childbearing by Teens: Links to Welfare Reform," and "Partners, Predators, Peers, Protectors: Males and Teen Pregnancy."

Child Welfare League of America (CWLA)
440 First St. NW, Third Floor, Washington, DC 20001-2085
(202) 638-2952 • fax: (202) 638-4004
e-mail: webweaver@cwla.org • website: www.cwla.org

CWLA develops and promotes policies and programs designed to protect America's children and strengthen America's families. Its member agencies provide a variety of services, such as child protection, kinship care, family foster care, adoption, and programs for pregnant and parenting teenagers. The league's publications include *First Talk: A Teen Pregnancy Prevention Dialogue Among Latinos, Facing Teenage Pregnancy: A Handbook for the Pregnant Teen,* and *The One Girl in Ten: A Self Portrait of the Teen-Age Mother.*

Coalition for Positive Sexuality (CPS)
3712 N. Broadway, Suite 191, Chicago, IL 60613
(773) 604-1654
website: www.positive.org

A grassroots volunteer group, CPS was formed by high school students to provide teens with sex-positive and safe sex information and to facilitate dialogue on condom availability and sex education. The CPS booklet *Just Say Yes*—written by teens for teens and available in English and in Spanish—addresses many issues concerning teen sexuality, including birth control, pregnancy, and abortion.

ETR Associates
PO Box 1830, Santa Cruz, CA 95061-1830
(831) 438-4060
website: www.etr.org

ETR Associates provides leadership, educational resources, training, and research in health promotion with an emphasis on sexuality and health education. The organization publishes a wide variety of health education resources, including books, flip charts, curricula, the pamphlet *Teens and Abstinence*, and the videotapes *Birth Control for Teens* and *First Things First: Teenage Relationships*. It also maintains the online Resource Center for Adolescent Pregnancy Prevention (www.etr.org/recapp), which provides practical, up-to-date tools and information to help teachers and health educators reduce sexual risk-taking behaviors in teens.

Family Research Council

801 G St. NW, Washington, DC 20001
(202) 393-2100 • fax: (202)393-2134
e-mail: corrdept@frc.org • website: www.frc.org

The council seeks to promote and protect the interests of the traditional family. It focuses on issues such as adolescent pregnancy and community supports for single parents. Among the council's numerous publications are the papers "Revolt of the Virgins," "Abstinence: The New Sexual Revolution," and "Abstinence Programs Show Promise in Reducing Sexual Activity and Pregnancy Among Teens."

Medical Institute

PO Box 162306, Austin, TX 78716-2306
(512) 328-6268 • fax: (512) 328-6269
e-mail: medinstitute@medinstitute.org
website: www.medinstitute.org

The institute works to inform, educate, and provide solutions to medical professionals, educators, government officials, parents, and the media about problems associated with nonmarital pregnancy and sexually transmitted disease. The institute advocates abstinence for unmarried individuals of all ages. Among its publications are the video *Just Thought You Oughta Know* and the brochures *Abstinence Because* and *Been There, Done That—Now What?*

National Campaign to Prevent Teen Pregnancy

1776 Massachusetts Ave. NW, Suite 200, Washington, DC 20036
(202)478-8500
website: www.teenpregnancy.org

The campaign's mission is to support cultural values and stimulate actions consistent with a pregnancy-free adolescence. It takes a public stand against teenage pregnancy and encourages others to do the same. The campaign's numerous publications include the manual *Get Organized: A Guide to Preventing Teen Pregnancy*, the pamphlet *Talking Back: Ten Things Teens Want Parents to Know About Teen Pregnancy*, the report "What About the Teens? Research on What Teens Say About Teen Pregnancy: A Focus Group Report," and the paper "Looking for Reasons Why: The Antecedents of Adolescent Sexual Risktaking, Pregnancy, and Childbearing."

National Organization on Adolescent Pregnancy, Parenting and Prevention (NOAPPP)

2401 Pennsylvania Ave. NW, Suite 350, Washington, DC 20037
(202) 293-8370 • fax: (202) 293-8805
e-mail: noappp@noappp.org • website: www.noappp.org

NOAPPP provides leadership, education, training, information, and advocacy resources and support to practitioners in adolescent pregnancy, parenting, and prevention. Members strive to address the issues of adolescent sexuality, pregnancy, and parenting at local, state, and national levels. In addition to the quarterly newsletter *NOAPPP Network*, the organization publishes such fact sheets as "Adolescent Pregnancy Statistics" and "Falling Teen Pregnancy Birthrates: What's Behind the Decline?"

Planned Parenthood Federation of America (PPFA)

810 Seventh Ave., New York, NY 10019
(212) 541-7800 • fax: (212) 245-1845
e-mail: communications@ppfa.org
website: www.plannedparenthood.org

PPFA works to ensure the right of individuals to make their own reproductive decisions. The federation promotes research and the advancement of technology in reproductive health care, provides comprehensive reproductive and health care services, and sponsors educational programs on human sexuality. PPFA also supports expanded sexuality education for teens and the development of contraceptive methods especially suited to adolescents. Its publications include the booklets *Birth Control Choices for Teens, Abortion: Commonly Asked Questions, Teensex? It's Okay to Say "No Way!"* and *What If I'm Pregnant?*

Sexuality Information and Education Council of the United States (SIECUS)

130 W. 42nd St., Suite 350, New York, NY 10036-7802
(212) 819-9770 • fax: (212) 819-9776
e-mail: siecus@siecus.org • website: www.siecus.org

SIECUS promotes comprehensive education about sexuality and advocates the right of individuals to make responsible sexual choices. The council maintains the Mary S. Calderone Library, which offers resource material on all aspects of human sexuality. SIECUS publishes and distributes diverse resources, including pamphlets, booklets, annotated bibliographies, the fact sheets "Teen Pregnancy" and "Adolescence and Abstinence," the bimonthly journal *SIECUS Report*, and the biweekly bulletin *SHOPTalk*.

BIBLIOGRAPHY

Books

Shirley Arthur — *Surviving Teen Pregnancy: Your Choices, Dreams, and Decisions.* Buena Park, CA: Morning Glory Press, 1996.

Janet Bode — *Kids Still Having Kids: Talking About Teen Pregnancy.* New York: Franklin Watts, 1999.

Phyllida Burlingame — *Sex, Lies, and Politics: Abstinence-Only Curricula in California Public Schools.* Oakland, CA: Applied Research Center, 1997.

Cynthia Cass — *Success After Teen Pregnancy: Against All Odds.* Kearney, NE: Morris, 1998.

Janet Ollila Colberg — *Red Light, Green Light: Preventing Teen Pregnancy.* Helena, MT: Summer Kitchen Press, 1997.

Robert Coles — *The Youngest Parents: Teenage Pregnancy as It Shapes Lives.* New York: W.W. Norton, 2000.

Joy G. Dryfoos — *Safe Passage: Making It Through Adolescence in a Risky Society.* New York: Oxford University Press, 1998.

Julie K. Endersbe — *Teen Fathers: Getting Involved.* Mankato, MN: Capstone Press, 2000.

Julie K. Endersbe — *Teen Mothers: Raising a Baby.* Mankato, MN: Capstone Press, 2000.

Julie K. Endersbe — *Teen Pregnancy: Tough Choices.* Mankato, MN: Capstone Press, 2000.

Melody Fleming — *Pregnant, Pissed, and Perplexed: A Pregnancy Prevention Guide for Curious Teens and Concerned Parents.* Indian Wells, CA: Creative Connections, 1999.

Tracey Hughes — *Everything You Need to Know About Teen Pregnancy.* New York: Rosen, 1999.

Jeanne Warren Lindsay and Jean Brunelli — *Your Pregnancy and Newborn Journey: A Guide for Pregnant Teens.* Buena Park, CA: Morning Glory Press, 1998.

Kristin Luker — *Dubious Conceptions: The Politics of Teenage Pregnancy.* Cambridge, MA: Harvard University Press, 1996.

Rebecca A. Maynard, ed. — *Kids Having Kids: Economic Costs and Social Consequences of Teen Pregnancy.* Washington, DC: Urban Institute Press, 1997.

Barbara A. Miller — *Teenage Pregnancy and Poverty: The Economic Realities.* New York: Rosen, 1997.

National Institute on Early Childhood Development and Education — *Compendium of School-Based and School-Linked Programs for Pregnant and Parenting Adolescents.* Washington, DC: U.S. Department of Education, February 1999.

Carolyn Simpson   *Coping with an Unplanned Pregnancy.* New York: Rosen, 1999.

Bernice Sparks, ed.   *Annie's Baby: The Diary of Anonymous, a Pregnant Teenager.* New York: Avon Books, 1998.

Gail Stewart   *Teen Fathers.* San Diego: Lucent Books, 1998.

Gail Stewart   *Teen Mothers.* San Diego: Lucent Books, 1996.

Gail Stewart   *Teen Parenting.* San Diego: Lucent Books, 2000.

Margi Trapani   *Reality Check: Teenage Fathers Speak Out.* New York: Rosen, 1999.

Periodicals

American Health Consultants   "Focus on Young Men in Pregnancy Prevention," *Contraceptive Technology Update,* August 1999. Available from 3505 Piedmont Rd. NE, Building #6, Suite 400, Atlanta, GA 30305-0056.

Link Byfield   "The Teen Sex Solution," *Alberta Report,* October 11, 1999. Available from 17327-106A Ave., Edmonton, AB T5S 1M7 Canada.

Janet Coburn   "Child Care in High Schools," *School Planning and Management,* January 1999. Available from 330 Progress Rd., Dayton, OH 45449-2322.

Francesca Delbanco   "Double Duty," *Seventeen,* April 1998.

Marilyn Gardner   "Shifts in Sex Ed: Talking Abstinence," *Christian Science Monitor,* August 11, 1998.

Cynthia Hanson   "Mom, I'm Pregnant," *Ladies' Home Journal,* August 1999.

Saul D. Hoffman   "Teenage Childbearing Is Not So Bad After All . . . Or Is It? A Review of the New Literature," *Family Planning Perspectives,* September/October 1998. Available from 120 Wall St., New York, NY 10005-3904.

Rebecca Lanning   "16 and Pregnant," *Teen,* September 1996.

Tamar Lewin   "Birth Rates for Teen-Agers Declined Sharply in the 90's," *New York Times,* May 1, 1998.

Marshall H. Medoff   "An Estimate of Teenage Abortion Demand," *Journal of Socio-Economics,* March/April 1999. Available from 100 Prospect St., PO Box 811, Stamford, CT 06904-0811.

People   "Revisiting 'The Baby Trap,'" October 11, 1999.

K. Lyne Robinson, James H. Price, Cynthia L. Thompson, and Hans D. Schmalzried   "Rural Junior High School Students' Risk Factors for and Perceptions of Teen-Age Parenthood," *Journal of School Health,* October 1998. Available from PO Box 708, 7263 State Rte. 43, Kent, OH 44240-0013.

Isabel V. Sawhill   "Welfare Reform and Reducing Teen Pregnancy," *Public Interest,* Winter 2000.

Deborah L. Shelton   "Does Sex Ed Focused on Abstinence Work?" *American*

Medical News, January 17, 2000. Available from 515 N. State St., Chicago, IL 60610-4325.

Julia Weeks Simanski   "The Birds and the Bees: An Analysis of Advice Given to Parents Through Popular Press," *Adolescence,* Spring 1998.

Joan Smith   "The Amazing Triumph of a Teenage Mom," *Redbook,* October 1999.

Sheryl Gay Stolberg   "U.S. Birth Rate at New Low as Teen-Age Pregnancy Falls," *New York Times,* April 29, 1999.

Kathleen Sylvester   "Preventable Calamity: How to Reduce Teenage Pregnancy," *USA Today,* March 1997.

Sylvia Pagan Westphal   "Partners of Underage Girls Focus of Study," *Los Angeles Times,* August 13, 1999.

INDEX